Jacob Laciar

Patriotism of Carbon County, Pa.

And what her people contributed during the war for the preservation of

the Union

.

Jacob Laciar

Patriotism of Carbon County, Pa.
And what her people contributed during the war for the preservation of the Union

ISBN/EAN: 9783337307769

Printed in Europe, USA, Canada, Australia, Japan

Cover: Foto ©Suzi / pixelio.de

More available books at **www.hansebooks.com**

GEN. CHARLES ALBRIGHT.

PATRIOTISM

OF

CARBON COUNTY, PA.,

AND

WHAT HER PEOPLE CONTRIBUTED DURING THE WAR
FOR THE PRESERVATION OF THE UNION.

BY J. D. LACIAR.

MAUCH CHUNK, PA.
1867.

PREFACE.

The object of the author of this volume, is the preservation of the names and services of the noble men, citizens of Carbon County, who served the country of their birth or adoption, during a period of danger, such as no nation ever experienced. The memory of the soldiers who saved the Republic of the United States from the destroying hand of a deeply-laid and long-premeditated Rebellion will be ever sacred in the hearts of the American people. It is due to the men who served faithfully in this great struggle, that their claims to the gratitude of their country should be distinctly recorded and preserved in a permanent form, so as to place it within the reach of all. It is with these views that the following record of the services of the Carbon County soldiers has been compiled. The author's aim has been to do justice to all, and as the greater portion of this work has been gathered from official sources, it is reliable and correct.

The companies are presented in the order of their organization, as near as possible. It will be observed that many names appear *twice*—such having re-enlisted. This is done in order not to mar the company organizations, and to present the rolls as they originally stood.

We have endeavored, at the expense of a great deal of labor and time to procure the name of every soldier from the county. But we do not pretend to have been successful in securing *every* one. We have simply done all we could, to make this work reliable and correct.

J. D. L.

The contributions of Carbon County in aid of suppressing the Slave-holders' Rebellion,—in proportion to her population,—is unequalled by any county in the State of Pennsylvania, and probably not surpassed by any community in any other State. Not only did this County furnish *more* men in proportion to her voting population, but the record of her soldiers is unsurpassed in point of bravery and endurance by any other troops. When the first call was made by President Lincoln for 75,000 troops for ninety days, Carbon County sent three full companies to Harrisburg in twenty-four hours. These companies were attached to the 6th Regiment Pennsylvania Volunteers. Immediately afterwards a full company was raised for three years, and attached to the famous "Bucktail Rifles." Upon the expiration of the three months' campaign two companies were raised for the 28th Regiment, P. V.; four Companies for the 81st Regiment, P. V.; one Company for the 67th Regiment P. V.; one Company for the 4th Pennsylvania Cavalry; one Company for the 11th P. V.; a portion of a Company for the 53d Regiment, P. V.; and a portion of a Company for the 11th Pennsylvania Cavalry. Besides these, about a Company were scattered in different other Regiments.

On the next call for troops, in 1862, two more full Companies were organized for nine months, which were attached to the 132d Regiment, P. V. When the State was threatened with invasion in 1862, a large number of men volunteered for the emergency. In 1863 when Pennsylvania was invaded, the county sent over four hundred men to repel the invaders. In 1864, over two hundred men volunteered for one year.— Besides these volunteers from the county, the different sub-districts paid bounties to the amount of hundreds of thousands of dollars to other volunteers.

The record of the Carbon soldiers commands the admiration of the country. From the beginning to the end of the war our gallant sons were at "the front." In Western Virginia— at Falling Waters—from the battle of Drainesville, in 1861, to the surrender of Johnson's army in 1865, there was scarcely a battle fought but witnessed the fall of some brave Carbon County soldier. On the Peninsula, where fell MILLER, CONNER, SHURLOCK, ABBOTT, and a host of others; at Chancellorsville, where the noble CHAPMAN sealed his devotion to his country with his heart's blood; at Bull Run, where the brave HYNDMAN died, fighting to the last; at South Mountain where BITTERLING cheered on his command with his last breath; at Mine Run, where we lamented the fall of PHILLIPS, at Spottsylvania, and in the long struggle for the capture of Richmond, where fell HAWK, GINDER, HOOVER, McGEE, PETERS and a host of others; in the last battle with Lee's army, where fell BOND, who had served from the very first call. At Gettysburg, Antietam, Fredericksburg, and a hundred other battle-fields where such men as Major Harkness, Captains Conner, Shields, Pryor, McLaughlin, Abbott, Marsh, Bieber, Patton and a thousand other brave Carbon County soldiers bled and won imperishable laurels.— In the struggles in the South-West, and in the long and fatiguing march of Sherman's army from Atlanta to the sea, in which many of the Carbon County men bled and died.—

Such men and such services have made up the Record which is presented in this volume.

While we point in sorrow to the long lists of the dead, we mourn with a pride which only such a record can inspire.— Such a record of heroism, where *five-eighths* of the soldiers sent from a community are killed and wounded. But, not only in bravery and heroic fighting is the record of these soldiers unequalled, but also in point of health and endurance. The grand record of casualties in the United States Volunteers during the war shows that double the number of soldiers died of disease as were killed in battle. The record contained in this volume, shows that THREE TIMES as many of the Carbon County Volunteers were killed in battle as died of disease. We give the record of officers, as follows :

One Brevet Brigadier General.

Three Colonels, of whom one was killed.

One Brevet Colonel, who was wounded.

Three Lieutenant Colonels, of whom one was killed and one wounded.

Three Majors, of whom one was killed and one wounded.

Twenty-eight Captains, of whom five were killed, one died and sixteen wounded.

Thirty-nine Lieutenants, of whom seven were killed and twenty wounded, making a total of seventy-eight officers furnished by Carbon County. Of this number FIFTEEN were killed, ONE died of disease, and thirty-nine wounded.

But it is not only the record of the officers that presents such unmistakable evidence of bravery and endurance. The men who filled the ranks have a record equally grand ; and it will stand for all time to come as a noble monument to the patriotism of little Carbon. While the remains of the loved ones rest peacefully in the dust of the battle-fields of the South; while we mourn the loss of so many of the noblest youths of our county; while fathers and mothers cherish the memory of patriotic sons, and widows and orphans that of husbands and fathers, we have the one proud consciousness that during a period of danger such as few nations have ever experienced, we were true to the legacy entrusted to us by the founders of this great nation. The people of Carbon county have the consciousness, that during the slave-holders' rebellion they discharged their whole duty.

Native and foreign alike served with honor and distinction, and it is but just to say of the German, Irish and Welsh, who form so large a proportion of the population of Carbon, that they came up nobly to the defence of their adopted country, and the list of deaths on many a battle-field attest the gallantry of the foreign portion of Carbon County Volunteers.

THREE MONTHS' VOLUNTEERS.

COMPANY "A," SIXTH REGIMENT, P. V.—Mustered into service APRIL 22, 1881. Discharged July 22, 1861.

Captain.—Eli T. Conner
1st Lieut.—Wm. I. Conner
2d Lieut.—John D. Bertolette

1st *Sergt.*—Edward D. Tombler		*Corporals.*—Alfred Knecht
2d " John T. Simpson		Delanson Geddas
3d " David Ginder		Oliver K. Pryor
4th " Charles Simons		Samuel D. Conner ·

Musicians.—Aquilla J. Marsh
Edward Wilson

Privates.—Andrews, Joseph
Angel, Abraham C
Arroman, John
Brelsford, Nathan
Bond, John
Bieber, Newton H
Briggs, Hiram
Briggs, Wm J
Briggs, Israel K
Conner, Thomas G
Ebert, Thomas W
Edwards, Richard
Ely, Ezra B
Foster, Henry
Grandison, Lewis
Hawk, Sidney N
Hawk, Samuel S
Horn, Edwin
Hanlin, Thomas
Henry, Aaron
Helmuth, Wm
Islan, John
Johnson, Andrew
Lynn, Nathan
Leffler, Nathan
Lines, Jesse
Langkammer, Charles
Long, Francis
Lindsay, John
Lesman, Ernst

Miner, Frank C
Millheim, John
Miller, Jacob
Moss, George W
McIntosh, Wallace
Moser, Aaron
Mank, Joel
Oxrider, Aaron
Ormrod, William
Patterson, James
Peltz, Charles H
Patton, John
Peters, Samuel
Painter, George F
Raw, Albert G H
Reinheimer, Daniel A
Richard Charles
Schadel, Joseph
Schofield, John M
Strittmaker, Frank
Schreiber, Lewis
Simpson, Wm
Smith, Wm
Tate, Robert
Tanner, Robert
Taggart, Stephen
Winters, Lebo
Walton, Alfred
Winner, Jacob
Will, Henry

Yonker, Benjamin.

Died.—Lentz, Alexander. Died in hospital at Hagerstown, Md., July 22d, 1861.

COMPANY "I," SIXTH REGIMENT, P. V.—Mustered into service
April 22, 1861. Discharged July 2?, 1861.

Captain.—John Craig
1st Lieut.—Samuel Shurlock
2d Lieut.—Wm. Belford

1st Sergt.—Thomas Kalbfus
2d   "   Nicholas C. Glace
3d   "   Wm. De Witt
4th   "   Lee Stiles

Corporals.—Wm. Miller
George Brown
Thomas B. Leisenring *
Wayne Winters

Musicians.—Charles Eberly
Charles T. Sigman

Privates.—Andre, Peter
Bloomy, Henry
Balentine, John
Boyd, W J
Burt, Andrew
Buer, Leonard
Buck, N
Beer, Wilson
Bellin, A S
Boyle, Peter
Boston, Robert
Brislin, John
Caffrey, James
Day, William
Dietrich, Henry
Dougherty, Peter
Dert. George
Frank. George **W**
Fink, Lewis
Goodman, Charles
Graham, John
Green, John
Gabriel, J E
Gilmore Archibald
Hanning, Frederick
Heaton, James
Hoover, Emanuel
Kindlin John
Knorr, Francis
Lewis, John
Lee. Joseph
Lindsay, Joseph
Long, Abraham

McDahola, Robert
Martin, Daniel
Mont, Adam
McCroty, John
Nagel, Jacob
Neimeyer, A C B
Overhold, C W
Overhold, S K
Pellea, John
Pearson, Otto
Petrie, Alexander
Peffercole, Henry
Reinmiller, Peter
Reed, Joseph
Rough, Abraham G
Rathwell, Joseph
Robison, James
Rutledge, John
Smith, Josiah
Seitzer, Washington
Smith, S S
Sheimer, A J
Saylor, Lewis
Stout, William
Shelheimer, J W
Smith, C D
Smith, James R
Sewell, John R
Thompson, Samuel
Thompson, J B
Yost, John
Yard, James.
Horne, Thomas

* Subsequently re-enlisted from Lehigh County, in the 47th Regiment. Promoted
to Captain, and served to the end of the war.

COMPANY "K," SIXTH REGIMENT, P. V.—Mustered into service April 22, 1861. Discharged July, 1861.

Captain —Thomas Wilhelm
1st Lieut.—Patrick Hughs
2d Lieut.—Jacob Arndt

1st Sergt.—Charles Cooper	Corporals.—Robert Depue
2d " James Warner	T. Siegfried
3d " Peter S. Ege	Henry F. Brown
4th " Daniel Tubbs	S K Austin

Drummer.—George H. Williams

Privates.—Arrowman, John
Acker, Cornelius
Buck, George
Bergenstock, Thomas
Billing, Joseph
Burnett, John
Brittain, John
Bowman, John
Briner, S
Buelow, John
Bowerfort, Martin
Barr, James
Conrad, Joseph
Conerty, Thomas
Connelly, Joseph
Chandler, D L
Call, Wm C
Derchun, Daniel
Dodson, E E
Dunbar, James
Fidler, John
Fritz, John
Flat, Franklin
Garrory, Wm
Glace, Henry R
Garritt, Wm R
Geddas, James
Henry Jonas
Hartz, David
Harris, William
Hoffman, Henry
Klotz, J J
Keefawber, Philip

Kleppner, C
Lewis, George
McQuire, John
McDawn, Owen
McGeehan, Daniel
Miller, S H
Miller, Thomas J
Murrier, Joseph
Munsen, Henry
Moore, Philip
Meacham, A
Minninger, C
Purcell, R S
Parkes, S C
Parker, Peter
Shultz, John
Shultz, Frederick
Shrank William
Schrœber, Frederick
Staples, Girard L
Sandherr, Anthony
Stone, A G
Sanrwine, Tilghman
Schucke, William
Slate, George
Summernian, Daniel
Smith, Joseph
Thomas, William
Williams, George
Wass r, J B
Watforce, Henry
Wharren, John
Young, E. D.

The Sixth Regiment Pennsylvania Volunteers was commanded by Colonel James Nagel, of Pottsville, Schuylkill County, and attached to General Patterson's Division, which served at Harper's Ferry, and on the Upper Potomac. A

very large proportion of the men in these companies, after
their discharge, enlisted for three years, or the war.   A large
number of them became officers.   Many are dead, as will be
seen by the lists of killed.

COMPANY "F,"—BUCKTAIL RIFLES.

PENNSYLVANIA RESERVE VOLUNTEER CORPS.

This Company was originally intended for the Campaign of three months, but when it reached Harrisburg no companies were accepted for a shorter term than three years. It was the first three years' organization at Harrisburg,—Mustered into service May 15, 1861.

Captain.—Dennis McGee.
> Commissioned May 15, 1861. Discharged in 1863, and subsequently reinstated, and resigned in 1865.

Sergeant.—Henry E. Swartz.
> Enlisted May 15, 1861. Discharged September, 1862—disability.

Sergeant.—George Seiwell.
> Enlisted May 15, 1861. Deserted from U. S. Hospital, 1862.

Sergeant.—W. Harry Rauch.
> Enlisted May 15, 1861. Served three years.

Sergeant.—George McIntosh.
> Enlisted May 15, 1861. Wounded at Drainesville, Dec. 20, 1861. Discharged September, 1862.

Armbruster, Fidel
> Enlisted May 15, 1861; re-enlisted January 3, 1864. Taken prisoner June 26, 1862, and May 3, 1864. Exchanged and served to end of the war.

Bott, George
> Enlisted August 6, 1861. Wounded at Drainesville, Dec. 20, 1861, and at Bull Run, August 30, 1862.

Beer, Philip
> Enlisted May 15, 1861. Wounded at Bull Run, August 29, 1862. Served three years.

Bierlingmeyer, George
> Enlisted December 16, 1861. Wounded at Antietam, September 17, 1862. Served three years.

Caden, John
> Enlisted May 15, 1861. Wounded at Bull Run, August 29, 1862. Served three years.

Curtis, William
Enlisted May 15, 1861.

Carr, Patrick
Enlisted May 15, 1861. Deserted.

Carroll, John
Enlisted May 15, 1861. Discharged on account of disability.

Deahn, John
Enlisted December 16, 1861. Re-enlisted and served to the end of the war.

Davis, Richard W.
Enlisted May 15, 1861. Discharged October, 1862, for disability.

Dugan, John
Enlisted May 15, 1861. Wounded at Fredericksburg, December13, 1862 and at the Wilderness, May 4, 1864. Re-enlisted and served to the end of the war.

Wierly, Joseph.
Enlisted May 15, 1861. Served three years.

Ehman, Frederick
Enlisted May 15, 1861. Wounded at Drainesville, December 20, 1861. Discharged May 1862.

Eickoff, George
Enlisted May 15, 1861. Served three years.

Eickoff, Ferdinand
Enlisted May 15, 1861. Wounded at Drainesville, December 20, 1861. Served three years.

Grieshaber, Anthony
Enlisted May 15, 1861. Served three years. Taken prisoner and exchanged.

Hawk, Lynford
Enlisted May 15, 1861. Wounded at Bull Run, August 29, 1862. Served three years.

Higgins, Edward
Enlisted May 15, 1861. Discharged on account of disability.

Henah, Michael
Enlisted May 15, 1861. Wounded at Charles City Cross Roads. Discharged.

Hettinger, William
Enlisted May 15, 1861. Wounded at Bull Run, August 29, 1862. Served three years.

Hills, John
Enlisted May 15, 1861. Wounded at Fredericksburg. December 13, 1862. Served three years.

Hollenbach, John
Enlisted July 21, 1861. Wounded at Bull Run, August 29, 1862. Re-enlisted and served to end of the war.

Herman, Albert
Enlisted May 15, 1861. Wounded at Charles City Cross Roads. Served three years.

Keiser, William
Enlisted May 15, 1861. Wounded at Fredericksburg, December 13, 1862. Served three years.

Kennedy, Patrick
Enlisted May 15, 1861. Wounded at Fredericksburg, December 13, 1862. Served two years and five months. Re-enlisted in another Regiment.

Meyer, John
Enlisted May 15, 1861. Wounded at Charles City Cross Roads. Served three years.

Matthews, James
Enlisted May 15, 1861. Wounded at Gaines' Mill. Re-enlisted and served to the end of the war.

Middler, Charles
Enlisted May 15, 1861. Wounded at Drainesville, December 20, 1861. Discharged on account of wounds.

McCafferty, John
Enlisted May 15, 1861. Discharged on account of disability, December 11, 1861.

Marshall, William
Enlisted May 15, 1861. Wounded at South Mountain, September 14, 1862. Discharged on account of wounds.

Quinn, Andrew
Enlisted May 15, 1861. Re-enlisted and served to end of the war.

Rhoads, Moses
Enlisted May 15, 1861. Discharged on account of disability, December 11, 1861.

Rehr, William F.
Enlisted May 15, 1861, Wounded at Gettysburg. Served three years.

Shannon, Philip
Enlisted May 15, 1861. Served three years.

Sutter, Frederick
Enlisted May 15, 1861. Wounded at Antietam, September 17, 1862. Discharged April, 1863.

Sellinger, Frank
Enlisted May 15, 1861. Wounded at Bull Run, August 29, 1862. Served three years.

Sullivan, Daniel
Enlisted May 15, 1861. Wounded and lost a leg at Fredericksburg, December 13, 1862. Discharged.

Scott, Thomas
Enlisted May 15, 1861. Re-enlisted and served to end of the war.

Trout, Charles
Enlisted May 15, 1861. Wounded at Bull Run, August 29, 1862. Discharged.

Vogel, Charles
Enlisted November 12, 1861. Discharged on account of disability.

Yanke, Theodore
Enlisted May 15, 1861. Discharged on account of disability.

Zundel, Henry
Enlisted May 15, 1861. Promoted to Chief Bugler. Served to end of the war.

LIST OF KILLED.

1st. Lieutenant.—Charles Bitterling.
Commissioned May 29, 1861. Killed in battle of South Mountain, September 14, 1862.

Sergeant.—Conrad Vogel.
Enlisted May 15, 1861. Killed in battle of South Mountain, September 14, 1862.

Corporal.—Joseph Shelly.
Enlisted August 16, 1861. Killed in battle of South Mountain, September 14, 1862.

Brannon, John
Enlisted May 15, 1861. Killed in the battle of Fredericksburg, December 13, 1862.

Brislin, Dennis
Enlisted April 29, 1861. Killed near Fredericksburg.

Connaghan, Andrew
Enlisted April 29, 1861. Killed at battle of Bethesda Church, May 30, 1864.

Fenstermacher, John
Enlisted May 15, 1861. Killed at battle of Gaines' Mill June 27, 1862.

Hanlin, Patrick
Enlisted May 15, 1861. Killed at the battle of Bethesda Church, May 30, 1864.

Hooker, John W.
Enlisted August 16, 1861. Wounded at Drainesville, December 20, 1861. Killed at Antietam, September 17. 1862.

King, Martin
> Enlisted August 6, 1861. Killed at the battle of the Wilderness, May 3, 1864.

McFadden, Charles
> Enlisted May 15, 1861. Killed at South Mountain, Sept. 14, 1862.

Mangold, Peter
> Enlisted May 15, 1861. Killed at South Mountain, Sept. 14, 1862.

McCue, Michael
> Enlisted May 15, 1861. Killed at Bull Run, August 29, 1862.

Munsen, Henry
> Enlisted December 16, 1861. Killed at the Wilderness, May 3, 1864.

Osman, John
> Enlisted July 21, 1861. Killed at Kelly's Ford, August 26, 1862.

Robins, William D.
> Enlisted May 15, '61. Killed at Charles City Cross Roads, June, 1862.

Shlaffley, Christian
> Enlisted May 15, 1861. Killed at Antietam, September 17, 1862.

DIED.

Fell, Stephen
> Enlisted May 15, 1861. Taken prisoner, and died a April, 1864.

Hollenbach, Samuel
> Enlisted July 21, 1861. Wounded at Fredericksburg, December 13, 1862. Re-enlisted. Captured and die. prisoner of war.

Schofield, Courtland
> Enlisted May 15, 1861. Died in Camp Pierpont, December, 1861.

Shiry, Stephen
> Enlisted May 15, 1861. Wounded at Bull Run, August 29, 1862, and died in rebel prison.

Shultz, Charles
> Enlisted December 16, 1861. Captured and died in rebel prison, in 1864.

The history of this company is identified with that of the noble Pennsylvania Reserves. The first action in which the Company participated was the skirmish at Falling Waters,

2

early in 1861. The first severe action was the battle of Drainesville, December 20, 1861. Subsequently the Company fought in the seven day's battle, on the Peninsula, in 1861; the battles of Bull Run, South Mountain, Antietam, Fredericksburg, Chancellorsville, Gettysburg, the Wilderness battles, and all through the long struggle to the front of Petersburg and Richmond in 1864. No organization rendered better service than Company "E," First Pennsylvania Bucktail Rifles.

28TH REG'T, PA. VOL'S.

COMPANY "E."—MUSTERED INTO SERVICE, JULY 6, 1861.—RE-ENLISTED DECEMBER 27, 1863. SERVED AS A COMPANY TO THE END OF THE WAR.

Major.—Jacob D. Arner.

    Entered the service as 1st Lieutenant, July 6, 1861. Promoted to Captain, January 15, 1863. Promoted to Major, June 1, 1865. Served to the end of the war.

Captain.—Simon F. Laurish.

    Enlisted June 25, 1861. Re-enlisted December 27, 1863. Promoted to 1st Sergeant May 1, 1863. Promoted to Captain in 1865. Severely wounded at the battle of Antietam September 17, 1862. Served to the end of the war.

First Lieutenant.—Charles F. Chapman.

    Commissioned 2d Lieutenant, July 6, 1861. Promoted to 1st Lieutenant, January 15, 1863. Served three years.

First Lieutenant.—Douglas McLean.

    Enlisted 1861. Re-enlisted in 1863. Promoted to Sergeant, September 1863. Severely wounded at Gettysburg, July 3, 1863. Promoted to 1st Lieutenant, 1865. Served to end of the war.

Second Lieutenant.—Frank McFall.

    Enlisted January 25, 1861. Discharged as Sergeant, December 1, 1862. Appointed 2d Lieutenant, Jan. 15, 1863.

Second Lieutenant.—Henry E. Grover.

    Enlisted in 1861. Re-enlisted in 1863. Promoted from Corporal to Sergeant, May 1, 1863. Promoted 2d Lieutenant 1865. Served to the end of the war.

Sergeant.—Bernhard Lynch.

    Enlisted in 1861. Re-enlisted in 1863. Promoted from Private to Corporal, February 18, 1863; to Sergeant, May 4, 1863. Served to the end of the war.

Sergeant.—Aaron Bennyhoff.
> Enlisted in 1861. Re-enlisted in 1863. Promoted from Private to Corporal, February 16, 1864; to Sergeant, April 1, 1865. Served to the end of the war.

Corporal.—George Harlos.
> Enlisted in 1861. Re-enlisted in 1863. Promoted to Corporal, July 1, 1863. Served to the end of the war.

Corporal.—Herbert Weston.
> Enlisted in 1861. Re-enlisted in 1863. Promoted to Corporal July 1, 1863. Served to the end of the war.

Corporal.—Gideon Moser.
> Enlisted in 1861. Re-enlisted in 1863. Promoted to Corporal, January 1, 1864. Served to the end of the war. Severely wounded at the battle of Ringgold, Ga., November 27, 1864.

Corporal.—Samuel Kunkle.
> Enlisted in 1861. Re-enlisted in 1863. Promoted to Corporal. January 1, 1864. Served to the end of the war.

Corporal.—Herman Ernst.
> Enlisted in 1861. Re-enlisted in 1863. Promoted to Corporal, January 1, 1864. Severely wounded at the battle of Mill Spring Gap, Ga., May 8, 1864. Served to the end of the war.

Corporal.—Jacob D. Fries.
> Enlisted in 1861. Re-enlisted in 1863. Promoted to Corporal, April 1, 1865. Severely wounded at Chancellorsville, May 3, 1863. Served to the end of the war.

Corporal.—Jacob Beers, Sen.
> Enlisted in 1861. Re-enlisted in 1863. Served to the end of the war.

Musician.—William Laird.
> Enlisted in 1861. Re-enlisted in 1863. Served to the end of the war.

Musician.—Michael McAllister.
> Enlisted in 1861. Re-enlisted in 1863. Served to the end of the war.

Wagoner.—John Fox.
> Enlisted in 1861. Re-enlisted in 1863. Served to the end of the war.

Amig, David
> Enlisted in 1861. Re-enlisted in 1863. Served to the end of the war.

Brennen, Richard
> Enlisted in 1861. Re-enlisted in 1863. Severely wounded at battle of Antietam, September 17, 1862. Served to end of the war.

Boyle, Edward
> Enlisted in 1861. Re-enlisted in 1863. Severely wounded at battle of Antietam, September 17, 1862. Served to end of the war.

Connerty, James
> Enlisted in 1861. Re-enlisted in 1863. Severely wounded at battle of Chancellorsville, May 3, 1863. Served to end of the war.

Davis, David B.
> Enlisted in 1861. Re-enlisted in 1863. Served to end of the war.

Henry, James
> Enlisted in 1861. Re-enlisted in 1863. Served to end of the war.

Johnson, William
> Enlisted in 1861. Re-enlisted in 1863. Served to end of the war.

Knecht, Thomas
> Enlisted in 1861. Re-enlisted in 1863. Served to end of the war.

Neith, Washington G.
> Enlisted in 1861. Re-enlisted in 18 3. Served to end of the war.

Pettit, Robert
> Enlisted in 1861. Re-enlisted in 1863. Served to end of the war.

Shaver, Henry J.
> Enlisted in 1861. Re-enlisted in 18 3. Served to end of the war.

Smith, William
> Enlisted in 1861. Re-enlisted in 1863. Served to end of the war.

Smith, Charles F.
> Enlisted in 1861. Re-enlisted in 1863. Served to end of the war.

Trout. Mabry
> Enlisted in 1861. Re-enlisted in 1863. Served to end of the war.

Weidaw, William
> Enlisted in 1861. Re-enlisted in 18 3. Severely wounded at the battle of Pine Knob, Ga., June 15, 1864. Served to end of the war.

DISCHARGED BEFORE THE END OF THE WAR.

Sergeant.—Moses Rehrig,
> Enlisted June 25, 1861. Discharged February 18, 1863, at Dumfries, Va., on account of disability.

Corporal.—Jacob Beers, Jr.
> Enlisted June 25, 1861. Discharged February 16, 1863, at Washington, D. C. Wounded in the foot, at battle of Antietam, September 17, 1862.

Corporal.—Oscar D. Case,
> Enlisted June 25, 1861. Discharged June 30, 1862, on account of disability.

Corporal.—David B. Shaffer,
> Enlisted June 25, 1861. Discharged February 18, 1863, on account of disability.

Corporal.—Alfred Wittingham,
> Enlisted June 25, 1861. Discharged December 31, 1862. Wounded and lost leg at battle of Antietam, September 17, 1862.

Corporal.—Jesse Gangewer,
> Enlisted August 27, 1862. Discharged May 18, 1865, by order of War Department.

Burns, John
> Enlisted June 25, 1861. Discharged July 20, 1864, having served enlistment of three years.

Curran, Patrick
> Enlisted June 25, 1861. Discharged June 23, 1862, on account of disability.

Campsie, Thomas
> Enlisted June 25, 1861. Discharged February 28, 1863, on account of disability.

Campbell, John
> Enlisted June 25, 1861. Discharged July 20, 1864, having served enlistment of three years.

Crilly, Francis
> Enlisted June 25, 1861. Discharged July 20, 1864, having served enlistment of three years.

Conover, John C.
> Enlisted December 23, 1861. Discharged Sept. 10, 1862.

Desmond, John
> Enlisted June 25, 1861. Discharged November 4, 1862. Disability.

Eisenbra, Frank A.
> Enlisted July 15, 1861. Discharged July 5, 1862. Disability.

Evans, Wm. H.
        Enlisted June 25, 1861.   Discharged July 20, 1864, having served three years.
Hamilton, Thomas
        Enlisted June 25, 1861.   Discharged February 28, 1862. Disability.
Hartley, Gustavus (Sergeant).
        Enlisted June 25, 1861.   Discharged July 8, 1864, having served three years.
Hummel, John H.
        Substitute.   August 16, 1864.   Discharged April 28, 1865, by order of the War Department.
Johnson, Solomon
        Enlisted June 25, 1861.   Discharged July 20, 1864, having served enlistment of three years.
Koons, Charles M.
        Enlisted June 25, 1861.   Discharged December 8, 1862. Disability.
Kinney, Peter L.
        Enlisted March 8, 1865.   Discharged June 27, 1865.
Labar, Jeremiah
        Enlisted June 25, 1861.   Discharged September 29, 1862.
Lentz, Henry
        Enlisted July 15, 1861.   Discharged July 20, 1864, having served out enlistment of three years.
Monroe, Robert S.
        Enlisted June 25, 1861.   Discharged July 20, 1864, having served out enlistment of three years.
McGadey, Edward
        Enlisted June 25, 1861.   Discharged July 20, 1864, having served out enlistment of three years.
McCue, Cornelius
        Enlisted June 25, 1861.   Discharged March 18, 1863.— Disability.
O'Brien, Thomas
        Enlisted July 15, 1861.   Discharged April 4, 1863.— Disability.
Odenkirchen, Peter
        Enlisted June 25, 1861.   Discharged July 20, 1864, having served out enlistment of three years.
Powels, James
        Enlisted June 25, 1861.   Discharged December 8, 1862. Disability.
Powels, Charles
        Enlisted June 25, 1861.   Discharged July 20, 1864, having served enlistment of three years.

Pratt, George W.
    Enlisted June 25, 1861.   Discharged March 10, 1863.—
    Disability.

Rudolph, William P.
    Enlisted October 27, 1862.   Discharged August 9, 1864.
    Disability.

Smith, Henry E.
    Enlisted June 25, 1861.   Discharged July 22, 1863, by
    order of the Secretary of War.

Sterling, Henry
    Enlisted June 25, 1861.   Discharged February 18, 1863.
    Disability.

Shutt, William B.
    Enlisted June 25, 1861.   Discharged February 24, 1863.
    Disability.

Thomas, Thomas G.
    Enlisted June 25, 1861.   Discharged November 29, 1862.
    Disability.

Weidaw, Aaron
    Enlisted June 25, 1861.   Discharged May 31, 1862.   Dis-
    ability.

Ward, Edward
    Enlisted July 15, 1861.   Discharged July 20, 1864, hav-
    ing served out enlistment of three years.

Walker, John J.
    Enlisted June 25, 1861.   Discharged June 3, 1862.

Young, Thomas
    Enlisted June 25, 1861.   Discharged May 16, 1865.   Vete-
    ran Volunteer.

Zehner, Joseph J.
    Enlisted June 25, 1861.   Discharged July 20, 1864, hav-
    ing served enlistment of three years.

TRANSFERRED.

Ackerman, John
    Enlisted June 25, 1861.   Transferred November 4, 1862,
    to 6th United States Cavalry.

Burns, Patrick
    Enlisted June 25, 1861.   Transferred July 1, 1863, to
    Invalid Corps.

Harris, Henry
    Enlisted June 25, 1861.   Transferred July 27, 1863, to
    Invalid Corps.

Jenkins, John
    Enlisted June 25, 1861.   Transferred October 5, 1861, to
    Knapp's Pennsylvania Battery.

Meyers, Casper S.
Enlisted June 25, 1861.   Transferred October 5, 1861, to Knapp's Battery.

Moody, William H.
Enlisted June 25, 1861.   Transferred October 5, 1861, to Knapp's Pennsylvania Battery.

Murphy, Patrick
Enlisted July 15, 1861.   Transferred August 13, 1863, to Invalid Corps.

McKiever, Isaac
Enlisted February 11, 1864.   Transferred April 21, 1865, to Veteran Reserve Corps.

Milhain, Charles
Enlisted June 25, 1861.   Transferred October 5, 1861, to Knapp's Pennsylvania Battery.

McGeady, John
Enlisted February 29, 1864.   Transferred January 1, 1865, to Veteran Reserve Corps.

Senn, Henry
Enlisted July 15, 1861.   Transferred November 4, 1862, to 6th United States Cavalry.

Yost, Gideon
Enlisted June 25, 1861.   Transferred November 15, 1863, to Invalid Corps.

RECRUITS.

Brindle, John
Enlisted March 21, 1864.   Veteran Volunteer.   Served to the end of the war.

Blowers, Hiram
Enlisted March 8, 1865.   Served to the end of the war.

Burie, John
Enlisted Feb'y 23, 1865.   Served to the end of the war.

Colbath, Oram
Enlisted Feb'y 27, 1865.   Served to the end of the war.

Compton, Thomas
Enlisted Feb'y 28, 1865.   Served to the end of the war.

Cortright, John P.
Enlisted March 6, 1865.   Served to the end of the war.

Dunbar, Elisha
Enlisted Feb'y 28, 1865.   Served to the end of the war.

Grover, Jacob W.
Enlisted Feb'y 9, 1864.   Served to the end of the war.

Gangewer, William
Enlisted Feb'y 15, 1865.   Served to the end of the war.

Major Langdon E. Chapman.

Hartz, David
Enlisted Feb'y 5, 1864. Served to the end of the war.

Kane, James W.
Enlisted Feb'y 4, 1864. Served to the end of the war.

Leinbach, William
Enlisted Feb'y 11, 1864. Served to the end of the war.

McCoy, William
Enlisted February 16, 1864. Severely wounded near Marietta, Georgia, June 20, 1864. Served to the end of the war.

Morris, Charles N.
Enlisted Feb'y 27, 1865. Served to the end of the war.

Peter, William H.
Enlisted March 8, 1865. Served to the end of the war.

Rawley, Caleb
Enlisted Jan. 29, 1864. Served to the end of the war.

Roth, Oliver W.
Enlisted Feb'y 27, 1865. Served to the end of the war.

Smith, David
Enlisted February 17, 1864. Served to the end of the war.

Scott, Robert
Enlisted February 4, 1864. Severely wounded near Marietta, Ga., June 20, 1864. Served to the end of the war.

Strohl, Thomas
Enlisted March 8, 1865. Served to the end of the war.

Wagner, Wesley
Enlisted February 28, '65. Served to the end of the war.

Wagner, William
Enlisted February 28, '65. Served to the end of the war.

Weaver, Clinton
Enlisted February 24, '65. Served to the end of the war.

Young, Charles
Enlisted February 2, '64. Served to the end of the war.

Yehl, Samuel
Enlisted February 27, '65. Served to the end of the war.

Graff, Isaac
Substitute. Feb. 7, 1865. Served to the end of the war.

KILLED.

Major.—Lansford F. Chapman,
Commissioned Captain, July 6, 1861. Promoted Major January 15, 1863. Killed in battle of Chancellorsville, Va., May 3, 1863.

Sergeant.—James Lynch,
> Enlisted June 25, 1861. Killed September 17, 1862, in the battle of Antietam, Md.

Sergeant.—Aaron Moser,
> Enlisted September 3, 1861. Died May 9, 1864, of wound received in battle at Mill Springs Gap, Ga., May 8, 1864.

Hertzogg, Daniel
> Enlisted June 25, 1861. Killed May 3, 1863, at battle of Chancellorsville, Va.

Hartz, Jacob
> Enlisted June 25, 1861. Re-enlisted as Veteran Volunteer, December 24, 1863. Died May 22, 1864, of wounds received May 8, 1864, at the battle of Mill Spring Gap, Ga.

Hagenbauch, William
> Enlisted June 25 1861. Re-enlisted as veteran volunteer. December 24, 1863. Killed June 15, 1864, at the battle of Pine Knob, Ga.

Johnson, James
> Enlisted June 25, 1861. Killed at the battle of Chancellorsville, May 3, 1863.

Nuss, Jacob
> Enlisted June 25, 1861. Died September 21, 1862, of wounds received at the battle of Antietam, Sept. 17, 1862.

Rawley, Harrison
> Enlisted June 25, 1861. Killed September 17, 1862, at the battle of Antietam.

Sauer, John
> Enlisted September 7, 1863. Died August 22, 1864, of wounds received in the battle of Peach Tree Creek, July 20, 1864.

Weiss, William
> Enlisted June 25, 1861. Re-enlisted as veteran volunteer December 24, 1863. Died July 10, 1864, of wounds received near Marietta, Ga., June 24, 1864.

DIED.

Brown, James
> Enlisted June 25, 1861. Died August 6, 1861, at Sandy Hook. Md.

Carey, William
> Enlisted June 25, 1861. Died May 22, 1862, in hospital at Alexandria, Va.

Eveland, Edward
> Enlisted June 25, 1861. Died May 10, 1863, at Acquia Landing, Va.

Gaumer, Franklin
> Enlisted June 25, 1861. Died May 10, 1862, at Rector-town, Va.

Moore, Robert
> Enlisted August 31, 1861. (Substitute.) Died August 31, 1864, at Bridgeport, Ala.

McKenna, Patrick
> Enlisted December 23, 1861. Drowned July 5th, 1862, while bathing in the Potomac at Bank's Ford.

COMPANY "A."

Simpson, William
> Enlisted as Drummer, June 1861. Re-enlisted in 1863. Promoted to Drum Major of the Regiment. Served to the end of the war.

Spohn, Frederick
> Enlisted June 1861. Promoted to Fife Major of the Regiment. Served three years.

147TH REG'T PA. VOL'S.

COMPANY "C."—Organized August 16, 1861.

[This was Company "N," 28th Regiment Pennsylvania Volunteers, previous to the organization of the 147th Regiment.]

Colonel.—John Craig.
> Commissioned Captain of Company "N," 28th Regiment, Pennsylvania Volunteers, August 30, 1861. Promoted to Major 147th Pennsylvania Volunteers, October 10, 1862; to Colonel, June 14, 1865.

Captain.—Nicholas C. Glace.
> Enlisted as 1st Sergeant, August 16, 1861. Promoted 2d Lieutenant, Feb'y 15, 1862; to 1st Lieutenant, Oct. 10, 1862; to Captain, March 1, 1864. Resigned July 22, 1864.

Sergeant.—John Kindelan.
> Enlisted in 1861. Served three years.

Sergeant.—William T. West.
> Enlisted in 1861. Re-enlisted and served to the end of the war.

Beer, Jacob
> Enlisted in 1861. Re-enlisted and served to the end of the war.

Black, Thomas
> Enlisted in 1861. Served three years.

Butler, William
>Enlisted in 1861.   Re-enlisted and served to the end of the war.

Dunham, Newman F.
>Enlisted in 1861.   Served three years as musician.

Gabrio, Joseph E.
>Enlisted in 1861.   Served three years as musician.

Green, A. Y.
>Enlisted in 1861.   Served three years.   Transferred to Knapp's Pennsylvania Battery, October 29, 1861.

Horn, Jacob
>Enlisted in 1861.   Served three years.

Kuntzman, Jacob
>Enlisted in 1861.   Re-enlisted in 1863.   Served to the end of the war.

Kresge, Andrew
>Enlisted in 1861.   Re-enlisted in 1863.   Served to the end of the war.

Mushart, Levi
>Enlisted in 1862.   Served to the end of the war.

Smith, Owen
>Enlisted in 1861.   Re-enlisted in 1863.   Served to the end of the war.

Shiner, John
>Enlisted in 1861.   Transferred to Knapp's Pennsylvania Battery, October 29, 1861.

Sebras, Philip
>Enlisted in 1861.   Discharged on account of Disability, January 3, 1863.

Steinmetz, William
>Enlisted in 1861.   Served three years.

Searls, George
>Enlisted in 1861.   Served three years.

Sayres, Emmett
>Enlisted in 1861.   Transferred to Veteran Reserve Corps.

KILLED.

Green, Aaron
>Enlisted in 1861.   Re-enlisted in 1863.   Killed in battle of Ringgold, Georgia, November 25, 1864.

Knoppenberger, Charles
>Enlisted in 1861.   Killed in battle of Antietam, September 17, 1862.

Kresge, Pauline
>Enlisted in 1861.   Re-enlisted in 1863.   Killed at Kenesaw Mountain, Georgia, 1864.

Sowers, John

Enlisted in 1861. Re-enlisted in 1863. Wounded at Pine Knob, Georgia. Died of his wounds, at Nashville, Tennessee, July 1854.

DIED.

Farres, William

Enlisted in 1861. Died at Falmouth, Virginia, in 1863.

Kent, John

Enlisted in 1861. Died at Alexandria, Va., in 1863.

Kents, Wayne

Enlisted in 1861. Died at Alexandria, Va., in 1863.

4TH REGIMENT PENNSYLVANIA VOLUNTEER CAVALRY.

COMPANY "A."

This company, although composed almost exclusively of Carbon County men, was, during the first two years of the war commanded by officers from other counties. Subsequently, however, the company produced some splendid and dashing officers. We are indebted to Captain William Hyndman for the very full and accurate history of this company.

Captain.—Joseph Andrews,

Enlisted August 7, 1861, as 1st Sergeant; promoted to 2d Lieutenant October 18, 1861, to 1st Lieutenant September 1, 1862; to Captain October 5, 1863. Mustered out of service September 20. 1864.

Captain.—William Hyndman,

Enlisted as private soldier, May 1, 1862; promoted to Corporal May 1, 1862; promoted to Sergeant July 31. 1863; to 1st Lieutenant December 13, 1864; to Captain March 8, 1865. Wounded at Upperville, Va., January 21. 1863; wounded and captured at Sulphur Springs, October 12, 1863. Escaped from Libby prison. Wounded March 27, 1865. Served to the end of the war.

Captain.—George W. Moss,

Enlisted August 7, 1861, as Sergeant; promoted to 1st Sergeant December 1, 1864; to 2d Lieutenant December 21, 1864. Promoted to Captain Company F, March 8, 1865. Wounded at Travillion Station, January 11, 1864. Served from the beginning to the end of the war.

First Lieutenant.—Herman Horn,
> Appointed 1st Lieutenant August 15, 1861. Resigned December 21, 1861.

Second Lieutenant.—Christian Freeby,
> Enlisted as private, August 7, 1861; promoted to Sergeant October 1, 1861; to 1st Sergeant December 4, 1861; to 2d Lieutenant September 1, 1862. Mustered out November 19, 1864.

Nathan Brelsford, (Sergeant.)
> Enlisted August 15, 1861. Re-enlisted and served to the end of the war.

Ash, Tilghman
> Enlisted August 15, 1861. Discharged August 15, 1864. Re-enlisted February 21, 1865. Served to the end of the war.

Arner, Reuben
> Enlisted February 29, 1864. Served to the end of the war.

Bloss, Daniel
> Enlisted August 15, 1861. Discharged, May 1, 1862, at Falmouth, Va., on account of disability.

Merrit A. Brown, (Bugler),
> Enlisted August 15, 1861. Discharged October 15, '62, at Philadelphia. Pa., on account of disability.

Robert Boston, (Sergeant).
> Enlisted August 15, 1861. Discharged July 20, 1863, at Harrisburg, by order of the Secretary of War.

Boyd, William J.
> Enlisted August 15, 1861. Discharged at Harrisburg, August 15, 1864, having served three years enlistment.

Bartholomew, George W.
> Enlisted February 16, 1864. Served to the end of the war. Wounded at Gravel Hill Farm, August 16, 1864.

Blakely, Tilghman
> Enlisted February 8, 1864. Transferred to Army of the West, December 29, 1864, by order of the Secretary of War.

Brown, Charles W.
> Enlisted Feb'y 20, 1865. Served to the end of the war.

Bobst, Charles
> Enlisted January 3, 1865. Served until disbandment of company.

Banks, Jacob
> Enlisted February 20, 1865. Served until disbandment of company.

Conner, Jos. C. H.
> Enlisted August 15, 1861. Re-enlisted and served to the end of the war.

Campsie, Alexander
Enlisted August 15, 1861. Re-enlisted and served to the
end of the war.

Cunning, Neal (Corporal).
Enlisted August 15, 1861. Re-enlisted and served to
the end of the war. Wounded at Dinwiddie Court House
March 31, 1865.

Conner, Wilfred
Enlisted February 29, 1864. Served to end of the war.

Crawford, Robert
Enlisted April 26, 1864. Served to end of the war.

Condon, Stephen
Enlisted August 20, 1864. Served to end of the war.

Dreisbach, Simon
Enlisted August 15, 1861. Discharged at Washington,
October 29, 1863, on account of Disability.

Drumbore, Joseph
Enlisted February 16, 1864. Served to end of the war.

Davis, James
Enlisted February 16, 1864. Served to end of the war.

Dugan, Hugh
Enlisted April 26, 1864. Served to end of the war.

Edwards, Richard
Enlisted August 15, 1861. Discharged August 15, 1864.
at Philadelphia, having served an enlistment of three years.

Edwards, Thomas
Enlisted August 15, 1861. Discharged August 15, 1864,
at Prince George Court House, Va., having served three
years.

Erwin, John
Enlisted August 15, 1861. Re-enlisted and served to
end of the war.

Edwards, Edward
Enlisted August 20, 1864. Served to end of the war.

Fritz, Nathan
Enlisted August 15, 1861. Discharged August 15, 1864,
at Philadelphia, Pa., having served three years.

Fidler, John
Enlisted August 15, 1861. Re-enlisted and served to
end of the war.

Furtwangler, Constantine
Enlisted February 15, 1865. Served until disbandment
of company.

Guth, John
Enlisted August 15, 1861. (Blacksmith.) Re-enlisted
and served to the end of the war.

Garvey, Nicholas

Enlisted August 15, 1861. Discharged August 15, 1864, at Prince George Court House, Va., having served three years. Wounded at Sulpher Springs, Va., October 12, '63.

Gallagher, Condy

Enlisted August 15, 1861. Discharged October 22, '64, near Petersburg, Va., having served three years. Captured in fight at Sulphur Springs, Va., October 12, 1863. Escaped from Andersonville prison, Ga., and succeeded in getting into our lines near Atlanta, Ga.

Gurlynn, Edwin

Enlisted August 16, 1864. Served to the end of the war.

Graver, William A.

Enlisted February 15, 1865. Served until disbandment of company.

Graver, Andrew

Enlisted February 15, 1865. Served until disbandment of company.

Haren, George

Enlisted September 1, '64. Served to the end of the war.

Hoffman, Alfred

Enlisted February 15, '65. Served to the end of the war.

Isley, John

Enlisted August 15, 1861. Re-enlisted and served to the end of the war.

Jeffries, John

Enlisted September 1, '64. Served to the end of the war.

Philip Keefaber, (Sergeant).

Enlisted August 15, 1861. Re-enlisted and served to the end of the war.

William Kain, Jr. (Sergeant).

Enlisted March 1, 1862. Re-enlisted and served to the end of the war. Wounded at Culpepper, September 13. 1863; wounded at Grant Hill Farm, August 16, 1864.

George Kent, (Corporal).

Enlisted August 15, 1861. Re-enlisted and served to the end of the war.

Knerr, Daniel

Enlisted February 20, '65. Served to the end of the war.

Kain, William, Sr.

Enlisted August 15, 1861. Discharged October 20, '62. Disability.

Klotz, William F.

Enlisted February 15, 1865. Served until disbandment of company.

Kopf, Francis Xavier
>Enlisted August 15, 1861. Discharged August 15, 1864, at Prince George Court House, having served out enlistment of three years.

Katzmoyer, Jacob
>Enlisted September 8, '64. Served to the end of the war.

Keck, Charles
>Enlisted September 29, 1862. Transferred to Veteran Reserve Corps, October 1863.

Kettra, Abraham
>Enlisted September 8, '64. Served to the end of the war.

Lewis, John J.
>Enlisted September 1, '64. Served to the end of the war.

Larish, Alfred
>Enlisted February 20, '65. Served to the end of the war.

Leslie, John
>Enlisted February 17, 1865. Served until disbandment of the company.

Moyer, Reuben
>Enlisted August 15, 1861. Discharged March 1. 1862. Disability.

Marcus Moyer, (Corporal.)
>Enlisted August 15, 1861. Discharged August 15, 1864, at Prince George Court House, Va., having served an enlistment of three years.

McMichael, Archibald
>Enlisted August 15, 1861. Re-enlisted and served to the end of the war.

McClean, Alexander
>Enlisted April 26, 1864. Served to the end of the war.

McLaughlin, Robert
>Enlisted August 15, 1861. Deserted March 1, 1862.

McHugh, John
>Enlisted August 16, 1864. Served to the end of the war.

Moore, Patrick
>Enlisted August 16, '64. Served to the end of the war.

Moore, James
>Enlisted September 8, 1864. Served to the end of the war. Wounded March 27, 1865.

McKeever, Thomas
>Enlisted September 8, 1864. Served to the end of the war. Served three years in 5th Regiment (loyal) Virginia Cavalry previously.

McLaughlin, Joseph
>Enlisted September 8, '64. Served to the end of the war.

3

McVay, Daniel
> Enlisted February 17, 1865. Served until disbandment of the company.

Miller, Henry
> Enlisted March 16, 1863. Served to the end of the war. Wounded in skirmish near Dumfries, Va., May 13, 1863.

Meyer, John
> Enlisted August 15, 1861. Transferred to Company B, Eleventh Pennsylvania Cavalry, August 24, 1861.

Nafts, Martzell
> Enlisted August 15, 1861. Re-enlisted and served to the end of the war. Wounded at Dinwiddie Court House, Va., March 31, 1865.

Oswald, William
> Enlisted August 15, 1861. Discharged August 15, 1864, at Prince George Court House, Va., having served an enlistment of three years.

O'Brien, Condy
> Enlisted February 17, 1865. Served until disbandment of company.

Patterson, Charles A.
> Enlisted August 15, 1861. Discharged January 1, 1862. Disability.

Powell, Samuel
> Enlisted February 16, 1864. Served to end of the war.

Richards, Thomas
> Enlisted February 16, 1864. Served to end of the war. Wounded March 27, 1865.

Richards, Jonathan
> Enlisted August 16, 1864. Served to the end of the war.

Rinker, John (Corporal)
> Enlisted August 15, 1861. Re-enlisted and served to end of the war.

Raw, Albert G. W. (Sergeant)
> Enlisted August 15, 1861. Re-enlisted and served to end of the war.

Smith, James (Sergeant)
> Enlisted August 15, 1861. Re-enlisted and served to end of the war.

Stermer, William
> Enlisted August 15, 1861. Discharged August 15, 1864, at Prince George C. H., Va., having served an enlistment of three years.

Thomas, William W.
> Enlisted August 20, 1861. Served to end of the war. Wounded March 27, 1865.

Thomas, David C.
    Enlisted September 1, 1864. Discharged May 20, 1865. on account of wounds received in action.

Welsh, John W.
    Enlisted August 15, 1861. Discharged February 8, 1865 on account of wounds received in battle. Lost a leg August 18, 1864.

Wertz, Peter
    Enlisted August 15, 1861. Re-enlisted and served to end of the war.

Younker, Benjamin S.
    Enlisted August 15, 1861. Transferred to Veteran Reserve Corps, December 15, 1864.

Zeigenfuss, Stephen
    Enlisted September 29, 1862. Re-enlisted and served to end of the war.

KILLED.

Hess, William T.
    Enlisted August 15, 1861. Killed at Gravel Hill Farm, Va., August 16, 1864. Parryville.

Brown, Miller H.
    Enlisted August 15, 1861. Killed at Fredericksburg. Va., December 13, 1862, while carrying dispatches to Gen. Hooker. Summit Hill.

Cochlin, Michael
    Enlisted August 15, 1861. Killed September 13, 1863, at Culpepper, Va. Summit Hill.

File, Jacob
    Enlisted August 15, 1861. Killed June 21, 1864, at St. Mary's Church, Va. Mauch Chunk.

Miller, George
    Enlisted August 15, 1861. Killed May 13, 1863 at Dumfries, Va. Summit Hill.

Weaver, John
    Enlisted September 8, 1864. Killed February 6, 1865, at Hatcher's Run, Va. Summit Hill.

Conner, Thomas
    Enlisted August 15, 1861. Died May 19, 1863, at Kelley's Ford, of wounds received in action. Weissport.

DIED.

Walton, Alfred (1st Sergeant)
    Enlisted August 15, 1861. Died in rebel prison at Andersonville, Ga., August 31, 1864. Captured at Sulphur Springs, October 12, 1863.

McLaughlin, James

Enlisted August 15, 1861. Died in rebel prison at Andersonville, Ga., August 20, 1864. Captured at Sulphur Springs, October 12, 1863.

Moyer, Gotleib

Enlisted August 15, 1861. Died in rebel prison at Andersonville, Ga., July 30, 1864. Captured at Sulphur Springs, October 12, 1863.

McCarren, John

Enlisted August 15, 1861. Died in rebel prison at Andersonville, Ga., July 28, 1864. Captured at Sulphur Springs, October 12, 1863.

Stahler, David

Enlisted August 15, 1861. Died in rebel prison at Andersonville, Ga., August 25, 1864. Captured at Sulphur Springs, October 12, 1863.

Smith, William

Enlisted August 15, 1861. Died in rebel prison at Andersonville. Ga., July 15, 1864. Captured at Sulphur Springs, October 12, 1863.

Shultz, John

Enlisted August 15, 1861. Died in rebel prison at Andersonville, Ga., July 30, 1864. Captured at Sulphur Springs, October 12, 1863.

Tiful, Richard

Enlisted August 15, 1861. Died April 30, 1863, at Dumfries, Va.

Bloss, Martin

Enlisted August 15, 1861. Died December 7, 1862, at Weissport, Pa., while at home on furlough.

Hand, Joseph

Enlisted August 15, 1861. Re-enlisted and died at Parryville, Pa., April 3, 1864, while on veteran furlough.

81st REG'T. PENNSYLVANIA VOLUNTEERS.

Colonel.—James Miller.

Commissioned Colonel August 8, 1861. Killed in battle of Fair Oaks, June 1, 1862.

Lieutenant-Colonel.—Eli T. Conner.

Commissioned Major October 1, 1861. Promoted to Lieutenant-Colonel June 1, 1862. Killed in battle July 1, 1862.

Captain.—Samuel Shurlock.

> Enlisted as Sergeant-Major, August 1861. Promoted to Captain Co. D. December 9, 1861. Killed June 15, 1862, while on picket duty.

Major.—Thomas McNeish.

> Commissioned 1st Lieutenant Co. I, October 15, 1861.— Transferred to the West and promoted to Major on Staff duty.

Lieutenant.—John Brelsford.

> Commissioned 1st Lieutenant and Quarter-Master, May 16, 1862. Severely wounded on the Peninsula in 1862.— Resigned in 1863.

COMPANY "G."

Lieutenant-Colonel.—Amos Stroh.

> Commissioned Captain, September 16, 1861. Promoted to Lieutenant-Colonel, April 17, 1863. Resigned.

Captain.—John W. Pryor.

> Commissioned 1st Lieutenant, September 16, 1861. Promoted to Captain of Co. D, February 28, 1863. Wounded at the battle of Allen's Farm, June 30, 1862; at Fredericksburg, December 13, 1862; at Gettysburg, July 3, 1863.— Resigned on account of his wounds, in 1864. Also, served during the Mexican War.

Captain.—Newton Bieber.

> Enlisted as 1st Sergeant in 1861. Promoted to Second Lieutenant, Jan. 1, 1862; to 1st Lieutenant, Co. F. Feb. 1, 1863; to Captain Co. C, Feb. 1, 1863. Wounded at the battle of Fair Oaks, June 30, 1862. Discharged August 24, 1863.

Captain.—John Patton.

> Enlisted in 1861. Promoted to 2nd Lieutenant, February 1, 1863; to 1st Lieutenant, February 28, 1863; to Captain in 1864. Wounded at the battle of Fredericksburg December 13, 1862, and at Gettysburg, July 3, 1863. Discharged in 1864.

Captain.—Nathan F. Marsh.

> Enlisted September 16, 1861. Re-enlisted in 1864. Promoted to Captain of Co. I, Jan. 7, 1865. Wounded in the battle of Gettysburg, July 3, 1863, and in battle in front of Petersburg, March 25, 1865. Served to end of the war.

1st Lieutenant.—Aquilla J. Marsh.

> Commissioned 2nd Lieutenant, September 16, 1861. Promoted to 1st Lieutenant, Co. A, Jan. 1, 1862. Resigned in 1863.

1st Lieutenant.—Lebo Winters.

> Enlisted in 1861. Promoted from Sergeant to 2nd Lieutenant, February 28, 1863. Promoted to 1st Lieutenant and served to end of the war.

Adams, William
> Enlisted in 1864. Wounded at Spottsylvania, May 1864.
> Served to end of the war.

Ashback, Jeremiah
> Enlisted in 1861.   Deserted from Hospital in September
> 1862.

Bond, George T.
> Enlisted in 1861.   Wounded on Peninsula in 1862. Dis-
> charged.

Brunner, Lewis
> Enlisted in 1861.   Wounded at the battle of Allen's
> Farm, June 30, 1862.

Brunner, John
> Enlisted in 1861.   Wounded in the foot at Harrison's
> Landing. Discharged.

Bachman, Griffith
> Enlisted in 1861.   Discharged on account of disability.

Bachman, Daniel
> Enlisted in 1861.   Discharged on account of wounds
> in October, 1862.   Lost a leg.

Bachman, Benjamin
> Enlisted in 1861.   Discharged on account of disability
> in May, 1863.

Brittain, William
> Enlisted in 1861.

Baker, Conrad
> Enlisted in 1861.   Wounded at Allen's Farm, June 30,
> 1862; at Fredericksburg, December 13, 1862.

Billinsby, John
> Enlisted in 1861.   Wounded at Allen's Farm, June 30,
> 1862.   Transferred to U. S. Artillery.

Brelsford, George W.
> Enlisted in 1861.   Severely wounded at the battle of
> Antietam, September 17, 1862.   Discharged on account of
> his wounds.

Bulkley, Henry
> Enlisted in 1861.

Bowman, Franklin
> Enlisted in 1861.   Discharged May 1863.

Campbell, Samuel
> Enlisted in 1861.   Wounded at Allen's Farm, June 30,
> 1862.   Discharged.

Connelly, Josiah
> Enlisted in 1861.   Transferred to U. S. Artillery.

Crilley, Oliver
    Enlisted in 1861.   Lost a leg in the battle of Antietam,
    September 17, 1862.   Discharged.

Derr, Obediah
    Enlisted in 1861.   Wounded at Antietam, Sept. 17, 1862,
    and at Fredericksburg, December 13, 1862.

Dorney, Nathan H.
    Enlisted in 1861.   Wounded at Fredericksburg, December 13, 1862.

Davis, William
    Enlisted in 1861.   Wounded on the Peninsula in 1862.

Doak, Henry
    Enlisted in 1861.

Edgar, James
    Enlisted in 1862.   Severely wounded at the battle of
    Gettysburg, July 2, 1863.   Discharged on account of his
    wound.

Frey, Miles J.
    Enlisted in 1861.   Served three years.

Eberts, William
    Enlisted in 1864.   Wounded at Spottsylvania, May 1864.
    Taken prisoner at Ream's Station.   Served to the end of
    the war.

Fenstermacher, Stephen
    Enlisted in 1861.   Wounded at Allen's Farm, June 30,
    1862.

Fields, Marshall
    Enlisted in 1861.

Fritz, Amon
    Enlisted in 1864.   Wounded at Spottsylvania, May 1864.
    Served to the end of the war.

Ginder, Jacob
    Enlisted in 1861.   Wounded at Gettysburg, July 3, 1863.
    Served three years.

Goodman, Henry
    Enlisted in 1861.   Discharged October, 1862.

Glace, William E.
    Enlisted in 1861.   Transferred to U. S. Artillery in 1862.

Geary, George
    Enlisted in 1864.   Wounded in front of Petersburg in
    1864.   Served to the end war.

Gombert, Jonathan H.
    Enlisted in 1861.   Lost arm in battle of Antietam, September 17, 1862.   Discharged.

Gallagher, Francis
> Enlisted in 1861. Wounded at Fredericksburg, December 13, 1862.

Gallagher, Patrick
> Enlisted in 1864. Served to the end of the war.

Gaumer, Alfred
> Enlisted in 1861. Wounded at Malvern Hill, June 30, 1862. Transferred to U. S. Artillery in 1862.

Horn, John
> Enlisted in 1861. Discharged in 1862, on account of disability. Re-enlisted in the 201st Regiment in February 1865, and served to the end of the war.

Hawk, Samuel
> Enlisted September 6, 1861. Discharged December 23, 1862. Re-enlisted.

Hollinger, Jacob A.
> Enlisted in 1861.

Hollinger, George, Jr.
> Enlisted in 1861. Wounded at Cold Harbor, June 3, 1864. Served to the end of the war.

Howard, James F.
> Enlisted in 1861.

Hontz, Amon
> Enlisted in 1861.

Hontz, Moses
> Enlisted in 1861.

Hontz, Charles
> Enlisted in 1864. Served to the end of the war.

Haggerty, Condy
> Enlisted in 1861.

Hammon, James
> Enlisted in 1861. Discharged from Hospital.

Hanning, Charles
> Enlisted in 1861.

Keller, Benjamin F.
> Enlisted in 1861. Wounded at the battle of Fredericksburg, December 13, 1862.

Kishbach, John
> Enlisted in 1861. Wounded at Fredericksburg, December 13, 1862.

Kuebler, Francis W.
> Enlisted in 1861. Served three years.

Kuebler, John
> Enlisted in 1861. Served three years.

Kramer, Wallace
>Enlisted in 1863. Wounded in front of Petersburg — Served to the end of the war.

Kirby, Michael
>Enlisted in 1861. Transferred to U. S. Artillery in 1862.

Koontz, John
>Enlisted in 1861.

Lovejoy, Alfred
>Enlisted in 1861. Discharged on account of disability in 1862.

Longkammer, Charles
>Enlisted in 1861. Wounded at the battle of Fair Oaks, June 1, 1862. Served three years.

Miller, William
>Enlisted in 1861.

McNeal, William
>Enlisted in 1861. Wounded at the battle of Antietam, September 17, 1862. Transferred to U. S. Artillery.

McGinley, Henry
>Enlisted in 1861. Wounded, and served three years.

Miller, Alexander
>Enlisted in 1864. Served to the end of the war.

McIntosh, George
>Enlisted in 1861. Wounded at Jerusalem Plank Road, June 22, 1864. Transferred to the Veteran Reserve Corps. Served to the end of the war.

Miller, Daniel
>Enlisted in 1864. Served to the end of the war.

Marsden, William
>Enlisted in 1861. Discharged in Hospital, October 1862.

McLean, Isaac
>Enlisted in 1861. Wounded at Antietam, September 17, 1862. Re-enlisted in 1864, and served to the end of the war.

Meaghan, Andrew
>Enlisted in 1861. Discharged on account of disability.

Martin, William
>Enlisted in 1861. Wounded at Fredericksburg, December 13, 1862.

McGowan, Michael
>Enlisted in 1861. Transferred to U. S. Artillery.

Mears, John E.
>Enlisted in 1861. Wounded and taken prisoner at Allen's Farm, June 30, 1862.

Meckes, William
>Enlisted in 1861. Deserted in 1862.

McGowen, James
Enlisted in 1861.

Moore, John
Enlisted in 1861.   Wounded at Fredericksburg, December 13, 1862.

Nothstein, Dennis
Enlisted in 1864.   Served to the end of the war.

Newton, John
Enlisted in 1861.   Wounded at Allen's Farm, June 30, 1862.

O'Donnell, Barney
Enlisted in 1861.   Wounded on the Peninsula, and at the battle of Antietam, September 17, 1862.

Oxrider, Lewis
Enlisted in 1861.   Wounded in the battle at Allen's Farm, June 30, 1862.

Pryor, Lewis
Enlisted in 1861.   Served three years.

Rough, Abraham
Enlisted in 1861.   Served three years.

Reinsmith, Nathan
Enlisted in 1864.   Wounded at Spottsylvania, May 1864. Served to the end of the war.

Rothrock, Charles
Enlisted in 1861.   Wounded in battles of Malvern Hill ; and at Fredericksburg. December 13, 1862.

Root, Manasses
Enlisted in 1864.   Served to the end of the war.

Reinsmith, Reuben
Enlisted in 1861.   Wounded in the battle of Malvern Hill, July 1, 1862.

Shive, Albert
Enlisted in 1864.   Wounded in front of Petersburg in 1864.   Served to the end of the war.

Strittmaker, Frank
Enlisted in 1861.   Re-enlisted and served to the end of the war.   Wounded by a guerilla while the army was returning to Washington May 1865.

Steinupe, ——
Enlisted in 1861.   Wounded at Fredericksburg, December 13, 1862.

Smith, Monroe
Enlisted in 1861.   Served three years.

Satorious, John G.
Enlisted in 1861.

Shæffer, Samuel
>Enlisted in 1861. Discharged.

Spinner, Andrew
>Enlisted in 1861. Wounded at Antietam, September 17, 1862.

Stein, John
>Enlisted in 1861. Deserted in 1862.

Smith, Peter
>Enlisted in 1861. Discharged.

Thompson, John
>Enlisted in 1861. Wounded at Gettysburg. July 2, 1863· Transferred to the Veteran Reserve Corps. Served to the end of the war.

Williams, William
>Enlisted in 1861. Wounded at Antietam, September 17 1862.

Winterstein, Samuel
>Enlisted in 1861.

Wallace, John
>Enlisted in 1861. Wounded at Fair Oaks, June 1, 1862. Re-enlisted in the 91st Regiment, P. V. Wounded in 1864.

Wissner, John
>Enlisted in 1861. Wounded at Malvern Hill. Discharged and subsequently died of his wound, at his home.

Wollinger, Joseph
>Enlisted in 1861. Wounded in the battle of Antietam, September 17, 1862.

West, George
>Enlisted in 1861.

West, John
>Enlisted in 1862. Wounded at Petersburg, June 16, 1864. Served to the end of the war.

Zellner, Henry
>Enlisted in 1861. Discharged on account of disability.

KILLED AND DIED OF WOUNDS.

Captain.—John Bond,
>Enlisted in 1861. Re-enlisted in 1863. Promoted to Captain of Company B. Killed in battle at Farmville, April 7, 1865.

Lieutenant.—Samuel Peters,
>Enlisted in 1861. Re-enlisted and promoted to Second Lieutenant. Killed in battle, June 17th, 1864, in front of Petersburg.

Lieutenant.—Peter McGee,

> Enlisted in 1861. Re-enlisted and promoted to Lieutenant of Company A, in 1864. Killed at the battle of Ream's Station, in 1864.

Ackerman, George

> Enlisted in 1861. Killed at the battle of Antietam, September 17, 1862.

Ege, Peter S.

> Enlisted in 1861. Killed in battle of Fredericksburg, December 13, 1862.

Geddes, Douglas

> Enlisted in 1861. Mortally wounded at the battle of Allen's Farm, June 30, 1862. Died in Libby Prison.

Gombert, William

> Enlisted in 1861. Killed at the battle of Fair Oaks, June 1, 1862.

Gallagher, Dennis

> Enlisted in 1861. Killed in battle of Antietam, September 17, 1862.

Gaumer, Frank

> Enlisted in 1864. Killed at the battle of Cold Harbor, June, 1864.

Haupt, John

> Enlisted in 1864. Killed at the battle of Spottsylvania, May 12, 1864.

Klotz, Francis

> Enlisted in 1864. Killed at the battle of Spottsylvania. May 12, 1864.

Medler, William

> Enlisted in 1861. Killed at the battle of Fredericksburg. December 13, 1862. ●

Moyer, Lewis

> Enlisted in 1861. Wounded at Malvern Hill, June 30. 1862. Killed at the battle of Fredericksburg, December 13, 1862.

Mullen, William

> Enlisted in 1861. Wounded at Fair Oaks, June 1, 1862. Killed in battle of Antietam, September 17, 1862.

Muckler, William

> Enlisted in 1861. Mortally wounded in battle of Fredericksburg, December 13, 1862. Died in hospital.

Nothstein, William

> Enlisted in 1864. Killed in battle at Spottsylvania, May 12, 1864.

Line, William

> Enlisted in 1861. Killed in battle of Fair Oaks, June 1, 1862. This is supposed to have been the first Carbon County soldier, killed in the rebellion.

Lomison, William
    Enlisted in 1861. Killed in battle of Antietam, September 17, 1862.
Shive, Samuel
    Enlisted in 1864. Killed in battle of Spottsylvania.
    May 12, 1864.
Sollinger, Paul
    Enlisted in 1864. Killed in battle of Spottsylvania.
    May 12, 1864.
Tubbs, Burton N.
    Enlisted in 1861. Wounded at the battle of Malvern
    Hill, July 1, 1862. Died of wound in rebel prison in
    Richmond.
West, Samuel
    Enlisted in 1861. Mortally wounded at Fredericksburg.
    December 13, 1862. Died at Point Lookout.

DIED.

Becker, Charles
    Enlisted in 1861. Died July 12, 1862.
Gormerly, John
    Enlisted 1861. Died in 1862.
McClellan, John
    Enlisted in 1861. Died at Turner Hospital, June 20, '62.
Overholser, Alfred
    Enlisted in 1861. Died at Newport News in 1862.

COMPANY "H."

Lieutenant Colonel.—Thomas C. Harkness,
    Commissioned Captain September 18, 1861. Promoted
    to Major, April 17, 1863. Promoted to Lieutenant Colonel.
    Wounded in several battles. Resigned.
Captain.—John C. McLaughlin,
    Commissioned First Lieutenant September 18, 1861 ;
    promoted to Captain Company "A," November 14, 1862.
    Severely wounded December 13, 1862, at the battle of
    Fredericksburg. Honorably discharged on account of
    wounds, June 12, 1863.
Captain.—Thomas Morton,
    Commissioned Second Lieutenant September 18, 1861 ;
    promoted to First Lieutenant November 14, 1862 ; to Cap-
    tain, April 17, 1863. Resigned in 1864.

Captain.—Thomas C. Williams,

Enlisted as First Sergeant, August 22, 1861; promoted to Second Lieutenant November 14, 1862; to First Lieutenant, April 17, 1863; to Captain, April 21, 1864.— Wounded in three battles, and discharged on account of his wounds.

First Lieutenant.—William J. Williams,

Enlisted in 1861 as Sergeant. Promoted to First Lieutenant, April 21, 1864. Served three years.

Lieutenant.—Stewart McIntosh,

Enlisted August 22. 1861. Re-enlisted and promoted to Lieutenant, 1865. Wounded at Ream's Station, and served to the end of the war.

Lieutenant.—Thomas Gallagher,

Enlisted August 22, 1861. Re-enlisted, and promoted to Lieutenant, 1865. Served to the end of the war.

Bell, James

Enlisted August, 1861. Wounded on the Peninsula, and at the battle of Fredericksburg, 1862. Served three years.

Breish, Aaron

Enlisted August, 1861. Taken prisoner on the Peninsula, 1862, and not heard from afterwards.

Blair, Hugh

Enlisted August 22, 1861. Re-enlisted, wounded, and served to the end of the war.

Boyle, Patrick

Enlisted August, 1861. Transferred to 4th U. S. Artillery in 1862. Served to the end of the war.

Brookmire, James G.

Enlisted August, 1861. Transferred to 4th U. S. Artillery in 1862.

Brannan, William

Enlisted August 22, 1861. Wounded and transferred to Invalid Corps.

Burns, James

Enlisted September 9, 1861. Deserted in 1864.

Cooper, Elijah

Enlisted September 9, 1861. Transferred to Invalid Corps.

Clemens, William

Enlisted September 9, 1861. Served three years.

Clark, John

Enlisted August 22, 1861. Re-enlisted and served to the end of the war.

Clark, James
> Enlisted August 22. 1861. Severely wounded at the battle of Fair Oaks, June 1, 1862. Discharged on account of his wounds.

Cokely, Patrick
> Enlisted in 1861. Transferred to U. S. Cavalry Regiment.

Cadden, James
> Enlisted in August, 1861. Wounded in battle. Served three years.

Coyle, Patrick B.
> Enlisted March 21, 1863. Deserted February 11. 1863.

Donahoe, Patrick
> Enlisted September 9, 1861. Wounded and taken prisoner May 10, 1864. Re-enlisted and served to the end of the war.

Dunn, Daniel
> Enlisted in 1861. Transferred to Band and discharged in 1862.

Evans, Jenkins
> Enlisted August, 1861. Wounded at Charles City Cross Roads, June 30, 1862. Discharged in 1863.

Eddie, William
> Enlisted August 9, 1862.

Elliot, William
> Enlisted August 22, 1861. Wounded at Charles City Cross Roads, June 30, 1862. Deserted in 1863.

Edwards, Owen
> Enlisted March. 1862.

Fritz, Charles
> Enlisted in 1861. Discharged in 1862, on account of disability.

Gallagher, John
> Enlisted in 1861. Discharged on account of disability in 1863.

Gallagher, Patrick (1st).
> Enlisted in 1861.. Wounded on the Peninsular in 1862. Re-enlisted and served to the end of the war.

Gallagher, Patrick (2nd)
> Enlisted March 21, 1862. Discharged February 11, '63.

Golden, Patrick
> Enlisted August 22, 1861. Discharged March 25, 1863, on account of wounds received at Fredericksburg, Dec. 13, 1862.

Henry, Aaron (1st Sergeant)
> Enlisted August 22, 1861. Wounded at the battle of Charles City Cross Roads, June 30, 1863, and at the battle of Bristow Station, in 1863. Served three years.

Hackett, Benjamin
> Enlisted in 1861. Transferred to the 4th United States Artillery, 1862.

Hewitt, William
> Enlisted in 1861. Wounded on the Peninsula in 1862, and transferred to the Veteran Reserve Corps.

Handline, Edward
> Enlisted in 1861. Accidentally wounded at Springfield Station, Va., and discharged.

Henry, John
> Enlisted in 1861. Wounded on the Peninsula, in 1862, and discharged.

Hughs, David
> Enlisted August 22, 1861. Wounded in the battle of Fredericksburg, December 13, 1862. Discharged April 15, 1863.

Jones, John T.
> Enlisted August 22, 1861. Wounded on the Peninsula in 1862. Discharged.

Jones, Charles W.
> Enlisted October 31, 1861. Wounded.

Kirk, James
> Enlisted August 22, 1861. Wounded on the Peninsula in 1862. Discharged February 26, 1863.

Kissner, William
> Enlisted August 22, 1861. Wounded in the battle of Charles City Cross Roads, June 30, 1862. Discharged on account of his wound.

Laughry, Hugh
> Enlisted August 22, 1861. Re-enlisted and served to the end of the war.

Lewis, John S.
> Enlisted August 6, 1862. Discharged on account of disability 1863.

Mackey, Robert
> Enlisted in 1861. Discharged in 1862.

Morgan, Thomas H.
> Enlisted in 1861. Deserted.

Morgan, Thomas T.
> Enlisted August 22, 1861. Taken prisoner in 1864, exchanged and discharged.

Mulhold, Thomas
> Enlisted August 22. 1861. Wounded at the battle of Fair Oaks, June 1, 1862, and discharged on account of his wound.

McLean, Daniel
> Enlisted in 1861. · Discharged on account of disability.

McFadden, John
> Enlisted August 6, 1862. Deserted January 12, 1863.

McMullen, Buchanan
> Enlisted in 1861. Deserted.

Murphy, James
> Enlisted in 1861. Discharged on account of disability, in 1863.

McCandles, Daniel
> Enlisted in 1861. Discharged on account of disability.

McNally, John
> Enlisted August 6, 1861. Discharged March 31, 1863.

Morrison, Charles
> Enlisted in 1861. Wounded on the Peninsula in 1862. Transferred to the 4th U. S. Artillery in 1862.

Nead, William
> Enlisted in 1861. Discharged on account of disability in 1863.

Powell, David
> Enlisted August 22, 1831. Wounded May 12. 1864.— Served three years.

Pugh, Howell
> Enlisted in 1861. Deserted.

Phillips, John
> Enlisted in 1861. Deserted.

Parker, John
> Enlisted March 21, 1862.

Quigley, John
> Enlisted August 1861. Wounded on the Peninsula in 1862. Discharged.

Quigley, William
> Enlisted August 22, 1861. Wounded May 10, 1864. Served three years.

Reese, Thomas
> Enlisted August 22, 1861. Transferred to Invalid Corps· Served three years.

Riley, Austin
> Enlisted in 1861. Deserted.

4

Reese, David
Enlisted in 1861.   Wounded on the Peninsula in 1862
Discharged on account of his wounds.

Robinson, Thomas
Enlisted August 22, 1861.   Lost a foot in the battle of
Cold Harbor, 1864.

Roberts, Robert
Enlisted August 29, 1862.

Stutz, Ernest
Enlisted in 1861.

Stephens, Vivian
Enlisted August 23, 1861.   Discharged September 29,
1862.

Snedden, Alexander
Enlisted August 23, 1861.   Wounded in the battle of
Gettysburg ; transferred to Invalid Corps, and served three
years.

Thomas, Philip
Enlisted August 22, 1861.   Wounded in the battle of
Gettysburg ; transferred to Invalid Corps. Served 3 years.

Thomas, Wm. T.
Enlisted in 1861.   Discharged on account of disability.

Vaughn, John
Enlisted March 18, 1862.

Wall, Christopher
Enlisted in 1861.   Wounded on the Peninsula in 1862.
Discharged on account of his wounds.

Williams, David
Enlisted August 22, 1861.   Served three years.

LIST OF KILLED AND DIED OF WOUNDS.

Delay, Jeremiah
Enlisted August 22, 1861.   Killed in battle of Charles
City Cross Roads, June 30, 1862.

Delamour, Wm.
Enlisted in 1861.   Killed at the battle of Charles City
Cross Roads, June 30, 1862.

Fisher, Owen
Mortally wounded in battle in front of Petersburg, 1864.
Died in Richmond.

Fritz, Michael
Mortally wounded at the battle of Charles City Cross
Roads, June 30, 1862.

Glenni, James
Enlisted August, 1861.   Mortally wounded at the battle
of Fredericksburg, December 13, 1862.

Laughry, James
> Enlisted September 9, 1861. Mortally wounded in battle, May 12, 1864. Died May 18, 1864.

Murry, James B.
> Enlisted in 1861. killed at Ream's Station, Va., August 25, 1864·

Murphy, Charles
> Enlisted August 22, 1861. Killed at the battle of Fredericksburg. December 13, 1862.

McLaughlin, Patrick
> Enlisted August 22, 1861. Killed at the battle of Charles City Cross Roads, June 30, 1862.

O'Donnell, John
> Enlisted August 22, 1861. Killed at the battle of Malvern Hill, July 1, 1862.

Ryemiller, Anthony
> Enlisted in 1861. Killed in battle at Charles City Cross Roads, June 30, 1862.

Radcliff, John
> Enlisted in 1861. Wounded on the Peninsula in 1862. Supposed to have been killed at Chancellorsville, May 3, 1863.

Reynolds, Edward
> Enlisted in 1861. Wounded at Chancellorsville, May 3. 1863. Mortally wounded in battle June 12, 1864.

Rogers, Andrew
> Enlisted in 1861. Killed at the battle of Charles City Cross Roads, June 30, 1862.

Williamson, Hugh
> Enlisted August 22, 1861. Killed at the battle of Fredericksburg. December 13, 1862.

Zimmerman, Emanuel
> Enlisted in 1861. Killed at the battle of Fredericksburg. December 13, 1862.

DIED.

Boyd, John
> Enlisted in 1861. Died in "Camp California," in 1862.

Beltz, Martin
> Enlisted in 1861. Died at Newport News in 1862.

Casey, William
> Enlisted in 1861. Died at Yorktown, 1862.

Davis, David E.
> Enlisted March 18, 1862. Died near Falmouth, Va., April 17, 1863.

Esbach, James W.
> Enlisted in 1861. Died in hospital at David's Island, New York.

Fitzpatrick, Patrick
> Enlisted September 9, 1861. Died in front of Petersburg, August, 1864.

King, James
> Enlisted in 1861. Taken prisoner in 1864; exchanged and died while home on furlough.

Swift, Richard
> Enlisted in 1861. Died in 1862.

COMPANY "I."

Captain.—William 1. Conner,
> Commissioned Captain, October 15th, 1861. Severely wounded in the Peninsula campaign in 1862. Again very severely wounded at the battle of Fredericksburg, December 13, 1862. Honorably discharged on account of his wounds, April 22, 1863.

Captain.—Joseph Webb,
> Enlisted in 1861. Promoted to First Lieutenant of Company A, 81st P. V.; promoted to Captain, April 8, 1865. Wounded in the Peninsula campaign in 1862.— Served to the end of the war.

First Lieutenant.—Thomas C. Hawk,
> Commissioned Second Lieutennut, October 15, 1861.— Promoted First Lieutenant, April 17, 1862. Wounded at the battle of Malvern Hill. Resigned November 24, 1862.

First Lieutenant.—Henry Paltzgrove,
> Enlisted in 1861. Re-enlisted in 1864. Wounded in the battles of White Oak Swamp, 1862, Fredericksburg, December 13, 1862, Cold Harbor, May, 1864. Promoted to Second-Lieutenant, May 13, 1864; 'to First-Lieutenant January 7, 1865. Served to the end of the war. Few soldiers have a brighter record.

Sergeant.—Oliver R. Pryor,
> Enlisted in 1861. Wounded severely. Re-enlisted in 1864, and served to the end of the war.

Sergeant.—William Moulthrop,·
> Enlisted in 1861. Severely wounded at the battle of Fredericksburg, December 13, 1862. Served three years.

Arp, George
> Enlisted in 1861. Discharged on account of disability.

Arp, Benjamin

Enlisted in 1861. Re-enlisted in 1864. Captured at the battle of Ream's Station, and imprisoned at Andersonville. Enlisted in the rebel army, November 29, 1864, and immediately afterwards escaped into the Union lines. Served honorably to the end of the war.

Burger, John

Enlisted in 1861. Re-enlisted in 1864. Served to the end of the war.

Bartholomew, Jacob

Enlisted in 1861. Re-enlisted in 1864. Wounded at Spottsylvania, May, 1864. Discharged on account of wounds.

Corn, Henry

Enlisted in 1861. Discharged on account of disability.

Campbell, John

Enlisted in 1861. Discharged on account of disability.

Everett, Thomas

Enlisted in 1861. Deserted from hospital.

Faulkner, Daniel

Enlisted in 1861. Discharged on account of disability.

Fell, Henry

Enlisted in 1861.

Glass, Peter

Enlisted in 1861. Discharged on account of disability. in 1862.

Gillespie, James

Enlisted in 1862. Wounded at the battle of Antietam.— Discharged on account of his wounds.

Hunsicker, William H.

Enlisted in 1861. Wounded on the Peninsula, and at the battle of Antietam in 1862. Discharged on account of his wounds.

Hall, Charles

Enlisted in 1861. Discharged on account of disability.

Hawk, Edward W.

Enlisted in 1861. Wounded in the Peninsula Campaign, in 1862. Discharged, and subsequently re-enlisted in the 183rd Regiment.

Hoffman, Henry

Enlisted in 1861. Discharged on account of disability.

Hains, William

Enlisted in 1861. Re-enlisted in 1864, and subsequently discharged.

Knause, Lewis

Enlisted in 1862. Transferred to Invalid Corps, in 1863.

Kresge, Frank
>Enlisted in 1861. Wounded in the Peninsula campaign, in 1862. Wounded and lost leg at Deep Bottom. Discharged in 1864.

Kramer, Wallace
>Enlisted in 1861.

Kenley, Charles
>Enlisted in 1861. Wounded in the Peninsula campaign, in 1862. Discharged in 1862.

Kemerer, Reuben
>Enlisted in 1862. Wounded at the battle of Deep Bottom, in 1864. Discharged.

Kline, Jeremiah F.
>Enlisted in 1861. Discharged on account of disability in 1863.

Leh, Francis
>Enlisted in 1861. Discharged on account of disability in 1863.

Long, Joseph H.
>Enlisted in 1861. Discharged on account of disability.

McMaster, John
>Enlisted in 1861. Deserted in 1862.

Miller, Mahlon
>Enlisted in 1861. Re-enlisted in 1864. Served to the end of the war.

Metzger, Samuel
>Enlisted in 1861. Re-enlisted in 1864. Wounded at the battle of Ream's Station. Served to the end of the war.

Milham, Thomas
>Enlisted in 1861. Discharged in 1863.

Owen, Frederick
>Enlisted in 1861. Discharged on account of disability in 1863.

Peters, Joseph M.
>Enlisted in 1861. Wounded at the battle of Charles City Cross Roads in 1862. Discharged on account of his wounds.

Romig, William
>Enlisted in 1861. Wounded and lost hand at the battle of Gettysburg. Discharged.

Raver, Henry
>Enlisted in 1861. Served three years.

Strouse, Jacob
>Enlisted in 1863. Wounded in battle in front of Petersburg, in June 1864. Served to the end of the war.

Stamitz, George
>Enlisted in 1861. Renlisted. Wounded in front of Petersburg Discharged on account of wounds.

Swartwood, Peter
Enlisted in 1861. Discharged on account of disability in 1862.

Snyder, Henry
Enlisted in 1861. Re-enlisted and served to the end of the war.

Shannon, William
Enlisted in 1861. Re-enlisted in 1864. Wounded at the battle of Cold Harbor, and served to the end of the war.

Sterling, John
Enlisted in 1861. Wounded in the Peninsula campaign in 1862. Re-enlisted and served to the end of the war.

Snyder, Frank,
Enlisted in 1861. Re-enlisted in 1864. Wounded at the battle of Gettysburg. Served to the end of the war.

Swob, William
Enlisted in 1861. Wounded at the battle of Fredericksburg, December 13, 1862. Discharged on account of his wounds.

Smith, Joseph
Enlisted in 1861. Wounded in the Peninsula campaign in 1862. Discharged on account of disability.

Taylor, William
Enlisted in 1861. Discharged on account of disability.

Timmons, Terrance
Enlisted 1861. Wounded at the battle of Antietam, September 17, 1862. Discharged on account of his wounds.

Unfriet, George
Enlisted in 1861. Discharged on account of disability in 1863.

Walker, Lorentz
Enlisted in 1861. Discharged on account of disability in 1862.

Youse, Israel
Enlisted in 1861. Served three years.

KILLED AND DIED OF WOUNDS.

Captain.—David J. Phillips,
Enlisted as Sergeant in 1861. Promoted to Second Lieutenant, September 1, 1862; to First Lieutenant and Adjutant, February 1, 1863; to Captain, April 22, 1863. Killed at the battle of Mine Run, December, 1863.

Captain.—David H. Ginder,

Enlisted as Sergeant in 1861; promoted to Second Lieutenant, February 1, 1863; to First Lieutenant, April 22, 1863; to Captain, December, 1863. Killed in front of Petersburg, June 17, 1864.

First Lieutenant.—Sidney N. Hawk,

Enlisted as Sergeant in 1861. Promoted to Second Lieutenant, April 22, 1863; to First Lieutenant and Adjutant, in 1864. Killed at the battle of Spottsylvania, May 12, 1864.

Second Lieutenant.—Hewitt J. Abbott,

Enlisted as Sergeant in 1861. Promoted to Second Lieutenant, April 17, 1862. Killed at the battle of Charles City Cross Roads, June 30, 1862.

Ackerman, James P.

Enlisted in 1861. Killed in the battle of Charles City Cross Roads, June 30, 1862.

Buck, Edwin

Enlisted in 1863. Killed in battle of Spottsylvania, May 12, 1864.

Dreisbach, Levi

Enlisted in 1861. Supposed to have been killed in front of Petersburg, June 16, 1864.

Flickinger, Thomas

Enlisted in 1861. Wounded at the battle of Charles City Cross Roads. Killed in the battle of Gettysburg, May 3, 1863.

Hopple, Jacob

Enlisted in 1861. Mortally wounded at the battle of Charles City Cross Roads, June 30, 1862. Died in Richmond.

Hinkle, Manville

Enlisted in 1861. Mortally wounded at the battle of Fredericksburg, Dec. 13, 1862.

Harris, Daniel

Enlisted in 1861. Killed at the battle of Charles City Cross Roads, June 30, 1862.

Kupp, Audelburg

Enlisted in 1861. Killed in battle in front of Petersburg, in 1864.

Miller, John

Enlisted in 1861. Killed at the battle of Charles City Cross Roads, June 30, 1862.

Nathan, Thomas

Enlisted in 1861. Killed at the battle of Charles City Cross Roads, June 30, 1862.

Peters, Charles E.

Enlisted in 1861. Killed at the battle of Fredericksburg, December 13, 1862.

Rader, David
>Enlisted in 1861.   Killed in the battle of Malvern Hill,
>in 1862.

Rehrig, Edwin
>Enlisted in 1861.   Killed in battle at Chancellorville,
>May 3, 1863.

Smith, Samuel
>Enlisted in 1861.   Killed at the battle of Charles City
>Cross Roads, June 30, 1862.

Whittingham, John
>Enlisted in 1862.   Killed in the battle of Fredericksburg.
>December 13, 1862.

DIED, AND STARVED IN REBEL PRISONS.

Buck, Owen
>Enlisted in 1861.   Wounded at the battle of Antietam,
>September 17. 1863.   Died in 1863.

Buskhart, Theophilus
>Enlisted in 1861.   Died on the Peninsula in 1862.

Conner, George
>Enlisted in 1861.   Died in 1861.

Durbert, John E.
>Enlisted in 1861.   Discharged and died in 1863.

Horn, James M.
>Enlisted in 1861.   Wounded in the battle of Charles City
>Cross Roads.   Wounded and taken prisoner at Ream's
>Station, August 25, 1864.   Died in Andersonville prison on
>the 11th of February, 1865.

Hains, Peter
>Enlisted in 1861.   Died in 1862.

Kugler, David
>Enlisted in 1861.   Died in 1862.

Laurish, Joseph
>Enlisted in 1861.   Died in 1862.

Lauer, Lafeyette
>Enlisted in 1861.   Taken prisoner at Ream's Station.
>August 25, 1864.   Died in Andersonville prison, January
>27, 1865.

Peters, Tilghman
>Enlisted in 1861.   Died in 1862.

Rader, Adam
>Enlisted in 1861.   Died in 1862.

Ruch, Charles E.
>Enlisted in 1861.   Taken prisoner at Ream's Station,
>August 25, 1864.   Died at Andersonville, January 17, '65.

Setzer, Harrison
>   Enlisted in 1861.—Died in 1862, at Alexandria, Va.

Whiteman, Joseph
>   Enlisted in 1862. Died in March, 1863.

TRANSFERRED.

Major.—Thomas McNeish,
>   Commissioned 1st Lieutenant October 18, 1861. Transferred to the Department of Tennessee, and promoted to the rank of Major.

COMPANY "K."

Lieutenant.—William Belford,
>   Commissioned Second-Lieutenant, October 27, 1861.—Discharged March 3, 1863.

Lieutenant.—Washington Setzer,
>   Enlisted as a private soldier in 1861. Re-enlisted and promoted to Lieutenant, January 7, 1865.' Served to the end of the war. Died at his home in Weatherly, July, '66.

Andreas, Abraham
>   Enlisted in 1862. Served to the end of the war.

Bond, George
>   Enlisted in 1861. Re enlisted and served to the end of the war. Wounded in battle.

Britt, John
>   Enlisted in 1864. Served to the end of the war.

Brindle, John
>   Enlisted in 1861. Discharged on account of disability in 1863.

Callaghan, William
>   Enlisted in 1864. Taken prisoner at Spottsylvania, and imprisoned at Andersonville.

Dougherty, John
>   Enlisted in 1861. Discharged on account of disability.

Farrow, Robert T.
>   Enlisted in 1862.

Farley, Michael
>   Enlisted in 1864. Served to the end of the war.

Fritz, J. C.
>   Enlisted in 1861. Discharged in 1863.

Hopkins, Lewis
>   Enlisted in 1861. Supposed to have died at Annapolis.

Kelly, Charles
Enlisted in 1864. Served to the end of the war.

Mulherren, Michael
Enlisted in 1864. Wounded at Poe River, not heard from afterwards.

Raver, Daniel
' Enlisted in 1861. Served three years.

Shoepp, A.
Enlisted in 1861. Discharged in 1862, on account of disability.

Washburn, Daniel
Enlisted in 1862. Wounded in the battle of Fredericksburg, December 13, 1862. Transferred to the Veteran Reserve Corps.

LIST OF KILLED.

Lieutenant.—Emanuel C. Hoover,
Enlisted in 1861. Re-enlisted in 1864. Promoted to Second-Lieutenant, and killed at the battle of Ream's Station, 1864.

Fellows, C.
Enlisted in 1861. Killed at the battle of Fredericksburg, December 13, 1862.

Matthews, Joseph
Enlisted in 1861. Killed at the battle of Fredericksburg, December 13, 1862.

Lowers, Penrose
Enlisted in 1861. Killed at the battle of Spottsylvania in 1864.

DIED OF DISEASE.

Andreas, John
Enlisted in 1862. Died at Falmouth, Va., December, '62.

Lutz, Thomas
Enlisted in 1861. Died on the Peninsula in 1862.

Stettler, Alexander
Enlisted in 1861. Died at Ship Point.

Washburn, Joseph
Enlisted in 1862. Died in service.

West, James
Enlisted in 1861. Re-enlisted and died in hospital, June 11, 1864.

LIEUT.-COL. ELI T. CONNER.

When the first proclamation was issued by President Lincoln, calling for troops, in 1861, Carbon County, like other communities, gave forth one great throe of patriotism. In the excitement of the moment, when hundreds were ready to follow, they cast about them for a LEADER,—who was capable of taking *command*. Captain ELI T. CONNER, at that time commanding officer of the "Anderson Grays," was acknowledged to be the man for the occasion, and to him the masses looked. He opened a recruiting office, and in twenty-four hours had recruited three full companies of the best young men of the county. He declined the offer of a field office, preferring to remain with his company. He served during the three months' campaign as senior Captain of the 6th Regiment Pennsylvania Volunteers.

Upon the expiration of his term of service, Captain Conner, (in connection with Colonel James Miller,) organized the gallant 81st Regiment, and on its completion was commissioned Major of said corps. On the Peninsula, he served with distinguished bravery, from the battle of Fair Oaks, to the final great and fearful struggle at Malvern Hill, where he fell. Immediately after the battle of Fair Oaks, Major Conner was promoted to Lieutenant Colonel, after which he commanded his regiment in all the battles during the campaign, until his death. Colonel Conner was born in Luzerne County, in 1832. His father, William Conner, settled in Mauch Chunk shortly afterwards, and died here in 1833. He was educated at Wyoming Seminary at Kingston, Luzerne County, and also subsequently attended a military school at Bristol, Pa. He was engaged as a civil engineer on the Lehigh Valley Railroad during the construction of the road, and was afterwards appointed Acting Engineer upon the slack water navigation of the Cape Fear River, in North Carolina, by Mr. E. A. Douglas. The climate not agreeing with him, he only remained in the south about a

COLONEL ELI T. CONNER.

year, and returned to Mauch Chunk.   Subsequently he again
entered the service of the Lehigh Valley Railroad Company,
and in the winter of 1859–60, he made the survey of the
Penn Haven and White Haven Railroad.

His first connection with the military of Carbon County
was as Lieutenant of the " Carbon Guards" at Summit Hill.
Having removed to Mauch Chunk, he was elected Captain
of the " Cleaver Artillerists," which position he filled with
much ability, until the fall of 1859, when the company was
disbanded, and a new company organized—the " Anderson
Greys," of which corps he was again elected Captain.   When
the war broke out, Captain Conner immediately signified his
determination to enter the service of his country, and nearly
every member of his company, with over two hundred
others followed him.

Kind, prompt, intelligent and brave, no better officer, or
truer friend to his country, fell during the war.

67TH REGT., PENNSYLVANIA VOLUNTEERS.

Colonel.—Horace B. Burnham.

> Commissioned Lieutenant-Colonel of the 67th Regiment
> August 12, 1861.   Participated with and most the time
> commanded his Regiment until January, 1864, when, hav-
> ing become incapable of further duty in the field, he was
> ordered to Washington, D. C.   On the expiration of his
> term of service, he was appointed by President Lincoln,
> Major and Judge Advocate U. S. Army, in the Department
> of New Mexico.   On March 13, 1865, he received two pro-
> motions, by brevet, conferring upon him the rank of Colo-
> nel, " for faithful and meritorious services, during the
> war."

COMPANY "I."

1st Lieutenant.—George W. Simpson.

> Commissioned September 24, 1861.   Captured at Win-
> chester, June 15, 1863, and remained a prisoner of war un-
> til March, 1865, part of which time he was, with a number
> of other prisoners, placed under fire of the Union guns, at
> Charleston, S. C,

Drum-Major.—John McArdel.
> Enlisted in November 1861.   Re-enlisted January, 1864.
> Served to the end of the war.

Callaghan, John
> Enlisted November 1861.   Served three years.

Dougherty, John
> Enlisted November 1861.   Re-enlisted January 1864.—
> Served to the end of the war.

Walton, Jesse
> Enlisted November 1861.   Re-enlisted January 1864.—
> Served to the end of the war.

COMPANY "A."

Captain.—David B. Burnham.
> Commissioned 1st. Lieutenant, August 12, 1861. Promo-
> ted to Captain November 9, 1863.

2nd Lieutenant.—Sylvester McCabe.
> Enlisted August 1861.   Promoted to 2nd Lieutenant
> February 20, 1862.   Honorably discharged March 17, 1863.

Sergeant.—Joseph Morris,
> Enlisted August, 1861.   Served three years.

Sergeant.—Daniel Zimmerman,
> Enlisted August, 1861.   Re-enlisted January, 1864.—
> Taken prisoner at the battle of Winchester, June 15, 1863.

Sergeant.—George Stocker,
> Enlisted August, 1861.   Taken prisoner at Winchester,
> June 15, 1863.   Served three years.

Sergeant.—William H. Siegfried,
> Enlisted August, 1861.   Taken prisoner at Winchester,
> June 15, 1863.   Served three years.

Corporal.—William Dunbar,
> Enlisted August, 1861.   Taken prisoner at Winchester,
> June 15, 1863.   Served three years.

Corporal.—Josiah Dotter,
> Enlisted August, 1861.   Missing after the battle of the
> Wilderness, supposed to have been killed.

Corporal.—Daniel Keiper,
> Enlisted August, 1861.   Wounded at Winchester, June
> 15, 1863.   Discharged on account of wound.

Corporal.—Jeremiah Trout,
> Enlisted August, 1861.   Taken prisoner at Winchester,
> June 15, 1863.   Wounded at the battle of the Wilderness,
> May 1864.   Served three years.

Corporal.—Melchoir Kintz,
Enlisted August, 1861. Taken prisoner at Winchester, June 15, 1863. Re-enlisted January, 1864, and served to the end of the war.

Corporal—George E. Williams,
Enlisted August, 1861. Taken prisoner at Winchester, June 15, 1863. Re-enlisted January 1, 1864.

Ague, John
Enlisted August, 1861. Taken prisoner at Winchester, June 15, 1863. Served three years.

Bartholomew, Michael
Enlisted August, 1861. Discharged in 1862 on account of disability.

Benner, John
Enlisted August, 1861. Wounded at Winchester, June 15, 1863. Discharged on account of wounds.

Berwick, Henry
Enlisted August. 1861. Wounded at the battle of the Wilderness, May 1864. Served three years.

Cailin, Patrick
Enlisted August, 1861. Re-enlisted January, 1864. Deserted.

Corrolus, Emlen L.
Enlisted August, 1861. Taken prisoner at Winchester, June 15, 1863. Re-enlisted and served to the end of the war.

Ditmire, Anthony
Enlisted August, 1861. Discharged in 1862, for disability.

Dunbar, James
Enlisted August, 1861. Taken prisoner at Winchester, June 15, 1863. Served three years.

Dotter, Lazarus
Enlisted August, 1861. Taken prisoner at Winchester, June 15, 1863. Served three years.

Dotter, Lewis
Enlisted August. 1861. Taken prisoner at Winchester. June 15, 1863. Served three years.

Eagen, Peter
Enlisted August, 1861. Taken prisoner at Winchester, June 15, 1863. Served three years.

Fritzinger, Levi
Enlisted August, 1861. Re-enlisted January 1864, and served to the end of the war.

Fitzpatrick, James
Enlisted August, 1861. Taken prisoner at Winchester, June 15, 1863. Served three years.

Green, Edward

Enlisted August, 1861. Wounded and captured at the battle of Winchester, June 15, 1863. Re-enlisted January 1864. Served to the end of the war.

Greensweig, Joseph

Enlisted August, 1861. Re-enlisted January 1, 1864, and deserted while on veteran furlough.

Goho, William

Enlisted in 1861. Deserted.

Greensweig, William

Enlisted August, 1861. Wounded and captured at Winchester, June 15, 1863. Re-enlisted January 1864, and deserted while on veteran furlough.

Greensweig, Thomas

Enlisted in 1861. Deserted in 1862.

Hawk, Jacob

Enlisted in 1861. Re-enlisted January 1864. Captured at Winchester, June 15, 1863. Served to the end of the war.

Hawk, Paul

Enlisted in 1861. Discharged for disability.

Heatherington, Irvin

Enlisted in 1861. Deserted.

Hawk, William

Enlisted in 1861. Wounded at the battle of Winchester, June 15, 1863. Discharged on account of wounds.

Higgins, John

Enlisted in 1861. Captured at Winchester, June 15, '63. Served three years.

Hartman, Charles

Enlisted in 1861. Deserted.

Hoot, John

Enlisted in 1861. Captured at Winchester, June 15, '63. Served three years.

Johnson, Andrew

Enlisted in 1861. Re-enlisted January 1864. Captured at Winchester, June 15, 1863. Served to the end of the war.

Kemerer, Daniel

Enlisted in 1861. Re-enlisted January 1864. Captured at Winchester, June 15, 1863. Served to the end of the war.

Long, Jacob S.

Enlisted in 1861. Served three years. Captured at Winchester, June 15, 1863.

Milheimer, John
        Enlisted in 1862. Served three years. Captured at Winchester June 15, 1863.

McGinnis, John
        Enlisted in 1861. Re-enlisted in January 1864, and deserted while on veteran furlough.

McCormick, Daniel
        Enlisted in 1861. Wounded and captured at Winchester June 15, 1863. Served three years.

Mann, Jacob
        Enlisted in 1861. Wounded and captured at Winchester June 15, 1863. Re-enlisted January 1864. Discharged in 1865.

Moyer, Daniel
        Enlisted in 1861. Wounded and captured at Winchester June 15, 1863. Served three years.

Mengle, Reuben,
        Enlisted in 1861. Captured at Winchester, June 15, '63. Served three years.

McVey, Daniel
        Enlisted in 1861. Captured at Winchester, June 15, '63. Served three years.

McFarland, John
        Enlisted in 1861. Re-enlisted January 1864. Deserted while on veteran furlough.

McFarland, Edward
        Enlisted in 1861. Wounded at Winchester, June 15,' 63. Re-enlisted and served to the end of the war.

Ross, Thomas
        Enlisted in 1861. Discharged in 1863.

Patterson, Charles
        Enlisted in 1861. Discharged in 1862.

Rader, Charles
        Enlisted in 1862. Captured at Winchester, June 15, '63. Served to to the end of the war.

Stocker, Phillip
        Enlisted in 1862. Captured at Winchester June 15, '63. Served to the end of the war.

Sterner, Reuben
        Enlisted in 1861. Discharged in 1862 for disability.

Seibler, George
        Enlisted in 1861. Captured at Winchester, June 15, '63. Re-enlisted January 1, 1864, and served to the end of the war.

5

Weiant, Samuel

Enlisted in 1861. Captured at Winchester June 15, '63. Re-enlisted and served to the end of the war.

Werner, Samuel

Enlisted in 1861. Served three years.

Wetzel, Gustavus A.

Enlisted in 1861. Served three years.

Wilson, Edward H.

Enlisted in 1861. Captured at Winchester June 15, '63. Re-enlisted and served to the end of the war.

Williams, Wm. P.

Enlisted in 1861. Discharged on account of disability in 1862.

LIST OF KILLED.

Captain.—Lynford Trock,

Commissioned 2nd Lieutenant, August 23, 1861. Promoted to Captain Co. H, February 20, 1862. Killed in battle of Winchester, June 15, 1863.

Color-Sergeant.—George W. Burton.

Enlisted August, 1861. Re-enlisted January 1864. Killed in battle near Winchester, September, 1864.

Corporal.—Hugh Collins.

Enlisted August 1861. Re-enlisted January 1864. Captured at Winchester, June 15, 1863. Killed in front of Petersburg, April 1, 1865.

Hanz, Jacob

Enlisted August, 1861. Killed at the battle of Winchester, June 15, 1863.

Materley, John

Enlisted August 1861. Killed at the battle of Winchester, June 15, 1863.

McKnelty, Patrick

Enlisted August, 1861. Killed at the battle of Winchester, June 15, 1863.

DIED.

Captain.—Jacob Arndt,

Commissioned Captain. August 28, 1861. Died at Philadelphia, November 8, 1863, from injuries received by being thrown from a horse.

Billman, Jacob

Enlisted August, 1861. Died at Annapolis, 1862.

Barnett, Mixsell

Enlisted August, 1861. Died at Annapolis, 1862.

Cantling, John
> Enlisted August, 1861. Re-enlisted in 1861. Died while on veteran furlough.

Jacoby, James
> Enlisted, August, 1861. Re-enlisted January, 1864.— Died in service.

Mulherren, Charles
> Enlisted in 1861. Re-enlisted, and died while on veteran furlough.

McEnrue, Owen
> Enlisted in 1861. Taken prisoner at the battle of the Wilderness. Died at Andersonville.

Scanlin, Joseph
> Enlisted in 1861. Re-enlisted January, 1864. Captured at the battle of the Wilderness. Died at Andersonville.

Welsh, William
> Enlisted August, 1861, Died in Philadelphia, December, 1861.

COMPANY "D."

Diehl, John
> Enlisted in 1861. Killed at the battle of Winchester, June 15, 1863.

COMPANY "H."

Hartman, Daniel
> Enlisted in 1861. Died July 7, 1864, in hospital.

53RD REG'T., PENNSYLVANIA VOLUNTEERS.

COMPANY "E."

Captain.—John Shields.
> Commissioned 1st Lieutenant, September, 1861 Promoted to Captain, February 23, 1863. Wounded at the battle of Fredericksburg, December 13, 1862. Severely wounded in the throat at the battle of Gettysburg, July 3, 1863. Discharged on account of his wounds, March 13th, 1864.

1st Sergeant.—Robert Tate.

> Enlisted September 1861. Wounded and captured at
> Savage Station; exchanged and rejoined his regiment.—
> Wounded and captured at the battle of Gettysburg, July 3,
> 1863. Remained a prisoner in the enemy's hands until the
> close of the war.

Sergeant.—James Hutchison.

> Enlisted October 1861. Re-enlisted and transferred to
> Veteran Reserve Corps in March, 1864. Served to the end
> of the war.

Sergeant.—Patrick Collins.

> Enlisted September 1861. Re-enlisted in 1863. Captured
> in front of Petersburg in 1864. Remained a prisoner until
> the close of the war.

Corporal.—P. F. Gildea.

> Enlisted September 1861. Transferred to the 1st U. S.
> Cavalry, October, 1862.

Corporal.—John McClelland.

> Enlisted September 1861. Wounded at the battle of
> Fredericksburg, December 13, 1862. Re-enlisted and served
> to the end of the war.

Boyle, Douglas E.

> Enlisted in 1861. Discharged in 1862. Re-enlisted in
> 202nd Regiment in 1864. Served to the end of the war.—
> Died after his discharge.

Collins, James

> Enlisted in September, 1861. Transferred to 1st U. S.
> Cavalry, October, 1862.

Davis, Job

> Enlisted in October, 1861. Discharged on account of
> disability in 1863.

Elliott, Condy

> Enlisted in September, 1861. Re-enlisted and served to
> the end of the war.

Gill, Peter

> Enlisted in September, 1861. Discharged on account of
> disability in 1862.

Meighan, John J.

> Enlisted in September, 1861. Transferred to 1st U. S.
> Cavalry in 1862.

McLaughlin, Patrick

> Enlisted September 1861. Re-enlisted and served to the
> end of the war.

O'Donnell, John

> Enlisted in September 1861. Transferred to 1st U. S.
> Cavalry in October, 1862.

KILLED.

Corporal.—Daniel McGinley,
> Enlisted in September, 1861. Killed in the battle of Fredericksburg, December 13, 1861.

Doyle, Peter
> Enlisted in September, 1861. Killed in the battle of Fredericksburg, December 13, 1862.

Heenan, Michael
> Enlisted in September, 1861. Killed in the battle of Fredericksburg, December 13, 1862.

DIED.

Beaty, Robert
> Enlisted in September, 1861. Died in hospital at New York, March 1863.

Conaghan, Patrick
> Enlisted in September, 1861. Died in hospital at Washington, D C., March 10, 1862.

Fitzgerald, James
> Enlisted in September, 1861. Died in hospital at Washington, March 10, 1862.

[Privates Andrew Conaghan, Dennis Brislin, and Patrick Hanlin, members of this company, were transferred to Company F. "Bucktail" Regiment, where their record is given. They were all killed.]

11TH REGIMENT PENNSYLVANIA CAVALRY.

COMPANY "H."

Captain.—Anthony Beers,
> Enlisted September 24, 1861. Re-enlisted January 1. 1864. Promoted from private to Corporal, December 17. 1861; to Sergeant, July 17, 1862; to 1st Sergeant, July 1. 1863; to Second Lieutenant, June 14, 1864; to Captain. February 13, 1865. Taken prisoner at Chapin's Farm. October 8, 1864, while acting aid to General A. V. Kautz. Paroled February 22, 1865. Served to the end of the war.

First Lieutenant.—Emery West,
> Enlisted September 24, 1861. Promoted from private to First Sergeant, July 17, 1862; to Second Lieutenant, July 1, 1863; to First Lieutenant, January 14, 1864. Mustered out October 18, 1864, having served three years.

First Lieutenant.—Philip B. Moore,

> Enlisted August 4, 1861; re-enlisted November 14, 1863.
> Promoted to Sergeant, March 28, 1864; Second Lieutenant,
> October 18, 1864; First Lieutenant, April 1, 1865. Served
> to the end of the war.

Second Lieutenant.—Simeon Albee,

> Enlisted September 24, 1861; re-enlisted November 18,
> 1863; promoted Corporal August 28, 1864; to Sergeant,
> September 9, 1864; First Sergeant, February 1, 1865;
> Second Lieutenant, April 1, 1865. Served to the end of
> the war.

Sergeant.—John Brighton,

> Enlisted September 24, 1861; re-enlisted November 13,
> 1863. Promoted Corporal, March 28, 1864; Sergeant,
> August 28, 1864. Severely wounded in an engagement
> near Richmond, December 19, 1864. Discharged August
> 13, 1865, from U. S. Hospital.

Bean, Daniel

> Enlisted September 24, 1861. Served enlistment of
> three years.

Christman, William

> Enlisted March 22, 1864. Served to the end of the war.

Frabel, Ephraim

> Enlisted March 22, 1864. Served to the end of the war.

Hall, Anthony

> Enlisted August 4, 1861. Re-enlisted January 1, 1864.
> Served to the end of the war.

Henning, Philip G.

> Enlisted September 24, 1861. Served three years.

Koons, William

> Enlisted September 24, 1861. Discharged January 29,
> 1862, on account of disability.

Keifer, William

> Enlisted September 9, 1861. Served three years.

Rose, George

> Enlisted March 8, 1864. Served to the end of the war.

Sandherr, Christian

> Enlisted December 19, 1863. Served to the end of the
> war.

Seagreaves, James G.

> Enlisted September 9, 1861. Discharged July 23, 1862.
> Disability.

Williams, George H.

> Enlisted September 24, 1861. Captured in an engage-
> ment near Carsville, Va., March 1863. Discharged at the
> end of the war. Deserted, and afterwards voluntarily re-
> turned.

Wilvert, Samuel
> Enlisted September 9, 1861.   Served three years.

KILLED AND DIED.

Sisty, Curtis F. (First Sergeant.)
> Enlisted August 17, 1861.   Re-enlisted January 1, 1864.
> Died while on furlough, at his home in Nesquehoning,
> January 28, 1865.

Bean, John (Corporal.)
> Enlisted September 23, 1861.   Re-enlisted January 1,
> 1864.   Was killed by guerrillas, near Smithfield, Va.. Feb-
> ruary 13, 1865.

West, Coursen (Corporal.)
> Enlisted August 4, 1861.   Mortally wounded by guer-
> rillas, August 31, 1862.   Died September 18, 1862.   This
> man was wounded while making a daring reconnoissance of
> the enemy's position at Black River.

COMPANY "A."

Edward Warner,
> Enlisted in 1864.   Served to the end of the war.

COMPANY "K."

W. S. Walter,
> Enlisted in 1864.   Served to the end of the war.

Henry Martin,
> Enlisted in 1864.   Served to the end of the war.

ANDERSON CAVALRY.

Jesse Jenkins, Josiah Warg, Benjamin Taylor.

75TH REG'T, PENNSYLVANIA VOLUNTEERS.

First Lieutenant.—William J. Briggs,
> Enlisted August 20, 1861.   Promoted Sergeant, Septem-
> ber 1, 1861; to 1st Sergeant, June 8, 1862; to 2d Lieuten-
> ant, September 15, 1863.   Acting Adjutant to the end of
> the war.

Sergeant.—William McGee,

Enlisted February 1864. Promoted Sergeant, August 20, 1864. Served to the end of the war.

Armbruster, Faldine

Enlisted February 1864. Served to the end of the war.

Beck, John

Enlisted February 1864. Served to the end of the war.

Ehman, Fritz

Enlisted February 1864. Served to the end of the war.

Fetch, John

Enlisted February 1864. Served to the end of the war.

Free, Harts

Enlisted February 1864. Served to the end of the war.

Shetzline, John

Enlisted February 1864. Served to the end of the war.

Smith, Andrew

Enlisted November 1861. Re-enlisted. Wounded at Gettysburg, July 1, 1863. Served to the end of the war.

11TH REGIMENT P. V. INFANTRY.

COMPANY "H."

Captain.—Daniel C. Tubbs,

Enlisted as 1st Sergeant. Promoted to 2nd Lieutenant, August 30, 1862; to Captain, June 20, 1863. Re-enlisted and served to the end of the war. Wounded in several actions.

2nd Lieutenant.—Josiah W. Fries.

Promoted to 2nd Lieutenant from Sergeant, June 30th, 1865, veteran volunteer, served to the end of the war.

Sergeant.—Samuel A. Wehr.

Enlisted October 15, 1861. Re-enlisted as veteran volunteer January 1, 1864. Wounded May 5, 1864. Served to the end of the war.

William Aubree, Musician.

Enlisted October 15, 1861. Re-enlisted January 1, 1864. Served to the end of the war.

Thomas Bobst, Wagoner.

Enlisted November 12, 1861. Re-enlisted January 1, '64. Served to the end of the war.

Cunningham, Terrance

Enlisted November 9, 1861. Re-enlisted January 1, '64. Served to the end of the war. Wounded in the campaign of 1864.

Kline, Charles
> Enlisted October 15, 1861.   Re-enlisted January 1, 1864.
> Served to the end of the war.

Moser, Joseph
> Enlisted October 15, 1861.   Re-enlisted January 1, 1864.
> Served to the end of the war.

Moyer, Lewis
> Enlisted December 13, 1861.   Re-enlisted January 1, '64.
> Served to the end of the war.

Mulligan, Thomas
> Enlisted October 15, 1861.   Mustered. out at the end of
> the war.

Poh, Henry
> Enlisted October 15, 1861.   Re-enlisted January 1, 1864.
> Served to the end of the war.

Reikert, John B.
> Enlisted October 15, 1861.   Re-enlisted January 1, 1864.
> Served to the end of the war.

Sandle, William
> Enlisted October 15, 1861. Served to the end of the war.

Weyhenmeyer, Eli
> Enlisted October 15, 1861. Re-enlisted January 1, 1864.
> Served to the end of the war.   Wounded.

HONORABLY DISCHARGED PREVIOUS TO END OF THE WAR.

Captain—E. H. Rauch.
> Enlisted October 15, 1861.   Discharged February 21st,
> 1863. Disability. Wounded at Bull Run, August 30, '62.

1st. Lieutenant—Henry Williamson.
> Enlisted October 15, 1861.   Discharged June 19, 1863,
> on accounts of wounds received in action.

1st Sergeant—Levi Miner.
> Enlisted October 15, 1861. Discharged February 4, 1863.
> Wounded.

Sergeant—Silas Solomon
> Enlisted October 15, 1861,   Discharged March 5, 1863.
> Received five wounds as the battle of Fredericksburg,

Corporal—John Seip,
> Enlisted October 15, 1861.   Discharged March 5, 1862.

Corporal—Herman H. Pryor,
> Enlisted October 15, 1861.   Discharged January 9, 1863.
> Wounded at Antietam, September 17, 1862.

Corporal—Anthony W. Raudenbush,
> Enlisted October 15, 1861.   Discharged March 27, 1863.
> Wounded at Fredericksburg, December 13, 1862.

Corporal—Daniel Houser,
    Enlisted October 15, 1861.   Discharged November 8, '64.
    Served three years.

Corporal—William Simpson,
    Enlisted October 15, 1861.   Discharged December 16th,
    1864. Served three years.

Musician—Irwin Miner,
    Enlisted October 15, 1861.   Discharged May 5, 1862.—
    Disability.

Wagoner—Thomas Arner,
    Enlisted October 15, 1861.   Discharged May 26, 1862.
    Disability.

Anthony, Mortimer
    Enlisted November 27, 1861.   Discharged October 31,
    1862. Under G. O. No. 102.

Battman, Emanuel
    Enlisted December 9, 1861.   Discharged March 10, 1863.
    Disability.

Blair, John
    Enlisted October 15, 1861.   Discharged June 15, 1865.
    Disability.

Craig, Robert
    Enlisted October 15, 1861.   Discharged January 15, 1863.
    Disability.

Collins, John H.
    Enlisted November 12, 1861.   Discharged November 13,
    1862. Disability.

Cregle, Tilghman
    Enlisted November 7, 1861.   Discharged January 15,
    1865. Disability.

Dennis, Franklin
    Enlisted November 7, 1861.   Discharged October 11,
    1862. Disability.

Erwin, Thomas
    Enlisted February 3, 1862.   Discharged June 9, 1864.—
    Wounded.

Fleming, Samuel
    Enlisted October 15, 1861.   Discharged February 18,
    1863. Disability.

Foulke, Charles
    Enlisted October 15, 1861.   Discharged October 24, 1863.
    Lost leg in action at Fredericksburg, 1862.

Haldeman, Christian
    Enlisted October 15, 1861.   Discharged September 23,
    1863. Lost leg in action at Gettysburg, July 1863.

Herring, Joseph
    Enlisted October 15, 1861. Discharged November 8, '64.
    Served three years.

Johnson, Isaac K. Sr.
    Enlisted October 15, 1861.   Discharged March 5, 1862.
    Disability.

James, E. James
    Enlisted December 17, 1861. Discharged March 13, 1862.
    Disability.

Knell, Joseph
    Enlisted October 15, 1861.   Discharged March 5, 1862.
    Disability.

Kistler, Daniel
    Enlisted December 16, 1861. Discharged June 16, 1865.
    Disability.

Loch, Jonas
    Enlisted November 22, 1861. Discharged April 25, 1862.
    Disability.

Lyon, Samuel
    Enlisted October 15, 1861.   Discharged January 13, '63.
    Wounds received at Antietam, September 1862.

McGinty, Bernard
    Enlisted October 15, 1861.   Discharged November 18,
    1861. Disability.

Miller, Henry J.
    Enlisted February 6, 1862.   Discharged November 28,
    1862. Disability.

Murphy, George
    Enlisted February 6, 1862. Discharged March 11, 1863.
    Disability.

McGeehan, Thomas
    Enlisted October 18, 1861.   Discharged January 11,
    1864. Disability.

Neith, Josiah
    Enlisted October 15, 1861. Discharged January 31, 1863.
    Wounded second battle of Bull Run, 1862.

Newhart, Benjamin F.
    Enlisted November 15, 1861. Discharged June 15, 1865.
    Disability.

Rose, George
    Enlisted December, 16, 1861.   Discharged October 17,
    1862. Disability.

Ray, William
    Enlisted October 15, 1861. Discharged December 28,
    1862. Wounded.

Radcliff, Lawrence
> Enlisted October 26, 1861. Discharged November 27, 1864. Served three years.

Sprohl, George
> Enlisted October 15, 1861. Discharged June 10, 1863. Disability.

Schneck, Elijah
> Enlisted December 17, 1861. Discharged January 17, 1863. Disability.

Wolf, William
> Enlisted October 15, 1861. Discharged February 17, '63. Disability.

Wintersteen, George W.
> Enlisted October 15, 1861. Discharged November 8, '64. Served three years.

Koch, John
> Enlisted October 15, 1861. Discharged June 13, 1865. Wounded at Gettysburg, July 1863.

Williams, Isaac
> Enlisted October 15, 1861. Discharged November 13, '62. Lost right hand at Antietam, Md., September 1862.

KILLED IN BATTLE, AND DIED OF WOUNDS.

Second Lieutenant.—James Hyndman,
> Enlisted October 15, 1861. Killed in action at Bull Run. Va., August 30, 1862.

Sergeant.—Thomas W. Ebert,
> Enlisted October 15, 1861. Killed in action at Gettysburg, Pa., July 1, 1863.

Corporal.—Lewis Grandeson,
> Enlisted November 9, 1861. Died, June 18, 1863: of wounds received in action at Bull. Run, August 30, 1862.

Adams, David
> Enlisted December 16, 1861. Killed in action at Gettysburg, Pa., July 1, 1863.

Boll, Lewis
> Enlisted November 12, 1861. Killed in action at Bull Run, Va., August 31, 1862.

Cunning, John
> Enlisted October 15, 1861. Killed in action at Fredericksburg, Va., December 13, 1862.

Deitrick, Josiah
> Enlisted December 13, 1861. Died, December 19, 1862, of wound received in action at Fredericksburg, Dec. 13, '62.

Folkmer, Edward
> Enlisted December 9, 1861. Killed May 6, 1864, in action at the Wilderness, Va.

Johnson, Matthew
Enlisted October 15, 1861. Killed in the battle of Gettysburg, Pa., July 1, 1863.

Lewis, John J.
Enlisted February 7, 1862. Killed in the battle of Bull Run, Va., August 39, 1862.

Lees, Benjamin
Enlisted October 15, 1861. Killed in the battle of Bull Run, Va., August 30, 1862.

Newmiller, Charles
Enlisted October 15, 1861. Died, October 13, 1862, of wound received in the battle of Antietam, September 17, 1862.

Poh, Josiah
Enlisted October 15, 1861. Killed in the battle of Gettysburg, Pa., July 1, 1863.

Waters, Peter
Enlisted October 15, 1861. Killed in the battle of Gettysburg, Pa., July 1, 1863.

DIED OF DISEASE, AND STARVED IN REBEL PRISONS.

Corporal.—Delanson Gaddes,
Enlisted February 18, 1862. Wounded in the battle of Bull Run, August 30, 1862. Taken prisoner at Weldon Railroad, August 19, 1864. Died in prison at Saulsbury. N. C., February 12, 1865.

Corporal.—James Black,
Enlisted October 15, 1861. Taken prisoner, August 19, 1864. Died February 10, 1865, in prison at Andersonville, Ga.

Gabriel, Schinke
Enlisted November 12, 1861. Taken prisoner on Weldon Railroad, August 19, 1864. Died in prison at Saulsbury. N. C., January 22, 1865.

Hoffman, Jeremiah
Enlisted October 15, 1861. Died of disease, November 13, 1862, at Washington, D. C.

Houser, Charles
Enlisted October 15, 1861. Died of disease, October 2, 1862, at Camp Parole.

Keef, John
Enlisted October 15, 1861. Killed by Accident, November 29, 1861.

Krum, Noah
Enlisted December 16, 1861. Died in Hospital of disease.

TRANSFERRED TO OTHER COMMANDS.

Lieutenant.—Samuel P. Lightcap,
> Enlisted October 15, 1861. Appointed Regimental Quarter-Master-Sergeant, October 1, 1864. Promoted to 1st Lieutenant and Quarter-Master, 1865.

Benhard, Lewis
> Enlisted October 15, 1861. Appointed Principal Musician of the Regiment, May 30, 1865.

Chester, Holden
> Enlisted December 13, 1861. Transferred to the Veteran Reserve Corps, July 24, 1863, on account of wounds received.

Davis, Isaac
> Enlisted October 15, 1861. Transferred to Veteran Reserve Corps, January 11, 1864.

Miller, Samuel
> Enlisted October 18, 1861. Transferred to the Veteran Reserve Corps, March 16, 1864, on account of wounds received at Gettysburg, July 1, 1863.

Snedden, Robert
> Enlisted October 15, 1861. Transferred to the Veteran Reserve Corps, July 1, 1863, on account of wounds received in action, September 17, 1862.

DESERTED.

Corporal.—William Kane,
> Enlisted October 15, 1861. Deserted December 1, 1862.

Delay, John
> Enlisted October 15, 1861. Deserted December 1, 1862.

Johnson, Isaac K. Jr.,
> Enlisted November 19, 1861. Deserted June 17, 1862.

Mattern, William
> Enlisted October 15, 1861. Deserted June 21, 1862.

2ND PENNSYLVANIA HEAVY ARTILLERY.

COMPANY "H."

Major.—Thomas Wilhelm,
> Commissioned Captain, December 19, 1861. Promoted to Major, November 25, 1862; acting Colonel commanding Provisional Regiment, Heavy Artillery, in 1864. Wounded at Cold Harbor, June, 1864. Commissioned Captain in Veteran Reserve Corps, at the end of the war.

Second Lieutenant.—Orlando Keene,
> Enlisted in 1851. Re-enlisted in 1863. Transferred to Company C, and promoted to Second Lieutenant in 1864. Served to the end of the war.

Sergeant.—Theodore P. Pryor,
> Enlisted in 1861. Served three years.

Sergeant.—Harry V. Morthimer,
> Enlisted in 1861. Served three years.

Sergeant.—Franklin C. Miner,
> Enlisted in 1861. Served three years.

Sergeant.—Cicero Wintermute,
> Enlisted in 1861. Served three years.

Sergeant.—George Slater,
> Enlisted in 1861. Served three years.

Brady, John
> Enlisted in 1861. Re-enlisted and served to the end of the war.

Corcoran, Christopher
> Enlisted in 1861. Transferred to Veteran Reserve Corps.

Koons, Willoughby
> Enlisted in 1865. Served to the end of the war.

Knecht, Alfred
> Enlisted in 1862. Served three years.

McGlynn, James
> Enlisted in 1862. Deserted.

Owens, Geo. C. P.
> Enlisted in 1862. Transferred to Veteran Reserve Corps.

Palmer, Francis
> Enlisted in 1862. Wounded at Chapin's Farm.

Smith, Wm. A.
> Enlisted in 1861. Served three years.

Smithers, Thomas
> Enlisted in 1861. Wounded at Petersburg, 1864

DIED.

Palmer, Edward
> Enlisted in 1861. Died at Hampton Hospital, 1864.

COMPANY "C."

Hatrick, Jonathan F.
> Enlisted December 2, 1863. Wounded at Chapin's Farm, September 29, 1864. Discharged January 29, 1866.

Bond, George T.
>>> Enlisted January 1864.   Discharged January 29, 1866.

Corcoran, Patrick
>>> Enlisted March, 1864.   Discharged January 29, 1866.

COMPANY "I."

Ferrie, Michael
>>> Enlisted in 1861.

Troy, Michael
>>> Enlisted in 1861.

Hawk, Samuel
>>> Enlisted in 1861.   Discharged on account of wound received in action.

132ND REG'T. PENNSYLVANIA VOLUNTEERS.

[Mustered into United States Service, August 15, 1862, for the term of nine months. Mustered out May 24, 1863]

Colonel.—Charles Albright,
>>> Commissioned Major, August 22, 1862; promoted to Lieutenant Colonel, September 28, 1862; promoted to Colonel, January 24, 1863.

COMPANY "F."

Captain.—J. D. Laciar,
>>> Enlisted as Second Lieutenant. Promoted to Captain, December 5, 1862. Slightly wounded at Antietam.

First Lieutenant.—Thomas Musselman,
>>> Slightly wounded at Fredericksburg, December 13, 1862.

Second Lieutenant.—John Kerns,
>>> Enlisted as Corporal. Promoted to Second Lieutenant, December 5, 1862.

SERGEANTS:

First Sergeant.—Oliver Breneiser,
>>> Wounded at the battles of Antietam and Fredericksburg.

Jacob Miller,   Charles Mack,
John Hoff,   John Sherry

CORPORALS:

Franklin C. Wintermute,   David M. Jones,

Albert E. Scheets,   William Miner,
William R. Rex,   Lewis Trainer,
    Sebastian Hahn, Wagoner.

PRIVATES:

Armbruster, Bartlett   Keene, Samuel
Allen, William   Kemerer, Edwin
Baker, Thomas   Moser, Francis H.
Cunfer, Stephen   McCance, Samuel
Christine, Thomas   Mattern, Monroe
Dreisbach, Charles S.   McGee, Daniel
Dreisbach, Joseph   Nothstein, Jacob
Everts, Peter   Neyer, Moses
Eck, Jonathan   Neumeyer, Val.
Fullweiler, Owen C.   Patterson, Charles A.
Frederick, Lewis   Rodfink, Jacob
Gumbard, Aaron H.   Rice, Leopold
Grow, Henry   Ridler, Jacob
Hough, Oliver   Solt, Paul
Hosler, Frederick   Siegfried, Wm. S.
Hottenstein, John W.   Sandell, Josiah
Houser, George   Steigerwalt, Monroe
Johnson, Alexander   Werstein, Henry

WOUNDED.

Corporal—John Shultz,
        Wounded at Antietam, September 17, 1862.

Arner, David
        Died at Summit Hill, Pa., after being mustered out of
    service.

Belsner, August
        Wounded at Chancellorville, May 3, 1863.

Everts, William
        Wounded at Fredericksburg, Va., December 13, 1862.

Fritz, Aaron
        Wounded at Fredericksburg, Va., December 13, 1862.

Frantz, William
        Severely wounded at Antietam, September 17, 1862.

Hontz, Joseph
        Severely wounded at Antietam, September 17, 1862.

Kistler, John
        Lost left arm in battle of Fredericksburg, Dec. 13, 1862.

6

Lynn, Samuel D.
>Wounded at Fredericksburg, Va., December 13, 1862.

Olwerstefler, Enos
>Wounded at Fredericksburg, Va., December 13, 1862.

Steigerwalt, Lewis
>Wounded at Fredericksburg. Va., December 13, 1862.

Sinker, Charles
>Wounded at Antietam, September 17, 1862.

Strouse, Jacob
>Wounded at Fredericksburg, Va., December 13, 1862.

DISCHARGED PREVIOUS TO EXPIRATION OF TERM OF ENLISTMENT.

Captain—George W. Wilhelm,
>Discharged, to date from December 5, 1862.

Seyfried, Edwin, Musician,
>Discharged February 25, 1863, on account of disability.

Drumbore, Joseph
>Discharged January 13, 1863, on account of wounds received in action at Antietam, September 17, 1862.

Everts, Samuel
>Discharged February 13, 1862, on account of disability.

Gearhart, George H.
>Discharged March 10, 1863, on account of wounds received in action. December 13, 1862.

Kressley, Daniel
>Discharged January 15, 1863, on account of disability.

Levy, Levi M.
>Discharged February 25, 1863, on account of disability.

Mills, Alexander
>Discharged September 25, 1862, on account of disability.

KILLED IN BATTLE AND DIED OF DISEASE.

Sergeant—Oliver F. Musselman,*
>Killed in the battle of Antietam, September 17, 1862.

Corporal—Joseph Shadel,
>Died November 28, 1862, at Belle Plains, Va., of disease.

---

*Sergeant Musselman possessed those beautiful traits of character which constitute the good soldier,—morality, intelligence, unflinching bravery, and devotion. Though only twenty years of age, his manly qualities had won for him the admiration and love of all who knew him. Generous and noble-hearted to a fault, his loss was deeply felt by his friends and companions in arms. In the bloody battle of Antietam, when his regiment was relieved, though already once wounded, he refused to leave the field, and joining with the Irish Brigade in one of their irresistible charges, he fell at the head of the column shot through the brain.

Grow, Samuel
> Died of wounds received in battle of Fredericksburg, December 13, 1862.

Moyer, Charles F.
> Killed in battle of Antietam, September 17. 1862.

Clewell, Joseph
> Died at Harper's Ferry, Va., of wounds received in action at Antietam, September 17, 1862.

Nace, James E.
> Died of wounds received in action at Fredericksburg December 13, 1862.

Lentz, John
> Died of wounds received in action at Fredericksburg December 13, 1862.

Ramaley, Charles W.
> Died January 27, '63, at Windmill Point, Va., of disease.

Rex, Aaron
> Died at Smoketown Hospital, November 11, '62. Wounded at Antietam.

Stermer, Otto
> Died March 25th, 1863, of wounds received in action at Fredericksburg, December 13, 1862.

Solt, Francis
> Died on the march in Maryland, about September 14, '62

DESERTED.

Duryea, George W.
> Deserted August 16, 1862, at Harrisburg.

Bartley, Daniel
> Deserted September 12, 1862, in Maryland.

COMPANY "G."

[Mustered into the U. S. Service, August 15, 1862, for the term of nine months. Mustered out May 24, 1863.]

Captain.—Isaac Howard,
> Promoted from Private to Captain, January 30, 1863.

First Lieutenant.—William H. Fulton,
> Promoted from Serg't to 1st Lieutenant, January 13. '63.

Second Lieutenant.—John Weiss,
> Promoted from Serg't to 2nd Lieutenant, March 17. '63.

SERGEANTS.

Charles Simons,	William Radcliffe,
Joshua Butler,	Charles Weiss.

CORPORALS.

Hugh Callan,   John Leslie,
William J. Springer,   Charles Bobst,
                David Garrret.

PRIVATES.

Abner, Charles   Lieser, Peter
Backert, Joseph   Leed, William
Connelly, Joseph   Mansfield, Henry
Cassady, Peter   Miller, Jonathan L.
Callaghan, William   Patterson, James
Davis, William   Poh, Alfred
Dempsey, Bernhard   Reilley, Michæl
Derbyshire, James   Reilley, Hugh
Dougherty, Michæl   Ronemous, Hugo
Earley, John   Sowerwein, Paul
Elliott, Patrick   Shæffer, David
Flemming, Patrick   Shingler, Jacob
Holmes, Charles   Smith, Bernhard
Hoy, William   Smitham, Thomas
Jenkins, Morgan   Synyard, Robert
Kinckle, Christian   Stacy, John
Kelley, Matthew   Schoonover, William
Kelley, Bernhard   Schoonover, Henry B.
Koltz, William F.   Weisley, John
Klotz, John F.   Weaver, Tilghman
Lange, Henry   Yemmons, Edward

WOUNDED.

Sergeant.—John T. C. Williams,
       Wounded at Antietam.
Corporal.—John Osborne,
       Lost leg in the battle of Chancellorsville, May 3, 1863.
Sprohl, Thomas
       Wounded at Antietam.

DISCHARGED PREVIOUS TO EXPIRATION OF TERM OF ENLISTMENT.

Captain.—Robert A. Abbott,
       Discharged January 13, 1863, on account of wounds re-
       ceived in the battle of Antietam, September 17, 1862.

First Lieutenant.—John Dolon,
> Discharged January 30, 1863, on account of disability.—
> Wounded at Antietam.

Second Lieutenant.—Edw. H. Salkeld,
> Discharged March 17, 1863.

Graver, John
> Discharged on account of disability.

Fry, Conrad
> Discharged on account of wounds, December 9, 1862.

Knouse, John
> Discharged on account of disability.

Koons, Willoughby
> Discharged on account of wounds received in the battle
> of Antietam, September 17, 1862.

Loch, Jonas
> Discharged on acccount of disability, December 24, 1862.

McGovern, John
> Discharged on account of wounds received in action, at
> Antietam, September 17, 1862.

Noble, William H.
> Discharged on account of disability.

Winterstein, Henry
> Discharged on account of wounds received in action, at
> Antietam, September 17, 1862.

Welsh, Michael
> Discharged on account of disability.

Youtz, Elijah
> Discharged on account of disibility, December 22, 1862.

KILLED IN BATTLE AND DIED OF DISEASE.

Darlington, Wilson M.
> Died January 31, 1863, of wounds received in action at
> Fredericksburg, December 13, 1862.

Ephlin, John
> Killed in the battle of Fredericksburg, December 13, '62.

Floyd, Andrew
> Died at Falmouth, Va., March 2, 1863, of disease.

Krum, William F.
> Died at Smoketown Hospital, Md., of wound received
> in action at Antietam, September 17, 1862.

McCullough, Michael
> Killed in action at Antietam, September 17, 1862.

Moyer, M.
> Died at Smoketown Hospital, Md., of wounds received in
> action at Antietam, September 17, 1862.

Mellick, Edward P.
>Killed in action at Antietam, September 17, 1862.

Ruch, Jonathan L.
>Died at Smoketown Hospital, Md., of wounds received in action at Antietam, September 17, 1862.

Solomon, John F.
>Died of disease October 1862.

DESERTED.

George Buck,   Rigby Thomas,
Luke Masterson,   John Toner,
George Rose,   Rufus Walters.

GENERAL CHARLES ALBRIGHT.

This officer attained the highest rank conferred upon any of Carbon County's soldiers. He is the only one of the large number of gallant officers who represented Carbon County in the army during the war, who attained a higher rank than that of Colonel. General Albright entered the army as Major of the 132nd Regiment P. V., his commission dating August 22, 1862. At the battle of Antietam, Md., four weeks later, he distinguished himself by unsurpassed coolness and bravery. On September 28th, 1862, he was promoted to Lieutenant Colonel, in which capacity he commanded his regiment through the valley from Harper's Ferry to the Rappahannock, and at the battle of Fredericksburg, December 13th, 1862. In this bloody conflict his indomitable courage and unflinching bravery won for him the most flattering encomiums from his Brigade and Division commanders. On the 26th of January, 1863, he was promoted to Colonel. During the winter and spring of 1863, he most of the time commanded a Brigade in the 3rd Division, 2nd Army Corps.

At the battle of Chancellorsville, in May, 1863, during the fierce fighting of the third day, Colonel Albright rendered splendid service with his little Brigade, in repelling the advance of the enemy.

The term of service of his regiment having expired shortly after this battle, he was mustered out, and returned to private life—which proved, however, to be of short duration.

Upon the invasion of Pennsylvania, in June, 1863, he immediately offered his services to the State, and organized the 34th Regiment Pennsylvania Militia. He was placed in command of Camp Muhlenberg at Reading, and subsequently was sent to Philadelphia, where he commanded until after the battle of Gettysburg, when his regiment was discharged, and he returned home. In August, 1864, when President Lincoln made his last urgent call for troops to re-enforce the struggling armies in the field, believing with all loyal men, that the time had come when a prompt out-pouring of the arm-bearing men of the North, would decide the war, Colonel Albright once more unsheathed his sword, and offered his services to the country. He received authority to organize the 202nd Regiment Pensylvania Volunteers, and in a very few days, had his regiment organized and equipped, and awaiting marching orders. When his regiment reached Alexandria, Colonel Albright was placed in command of the line of the Orange and Alexandria Railroad, between Rector-town and White Plains, Va. During the rebellion there was probably no more disagreeable position for an officer to be placed into, than that of governing a country, infested by guerrillas, where all species of outrages were daily committed by those bands of desperadoes. The section of country which Colonel Albright was placed in command of, being the guerilla Moseby's favorite stamping ground, promised an active field. The lenient policy which had heretofore encouraged all manner of infamies by the guerrilla inhabitants of this section of the country, immediately gave way to the firm and decided measures adopted by Colonel Albright, and soon these guerrilla outrages became less frequent, and finally ceased almost altogether.

When the Orange and Alexandria Railroad was finally abandoned by the Government, Colonel Albright was placed in command of Fairfax Station, and shortly afterwards commenced the construction of elaborate fortifications at that place, which were completed shortly before the surrender of Lee's Army. While in command of this post, his services to his country were partially rewarded by a brevet promotion to BRIGADIER GENERAL.

While stationed at this point, General Albright learned that a body of Moseby's guerrillas, several hundred strong, intended to surprise and capture a large wagon train, a few miles from Fairfax Station. He immediately ordered out a squadron of the 8th Illinois Cav-

alry—which was attached to his command—and intercepted
the enemy near Wolf Run Shoals, and compelled him to give
battle. After several charges, in which General Albright led
his command in person, he succeeded in routing the rebels—
killing, wounding, and capturing a considerable number of
men and horses. In this gallant fight General Albright dis-
played that dashing courage which characterized him in all
the engagements in which he participated. Dashing into the
midst of them and discharging his pistols almost in the faces
of the enemy. By his promptness and energy, and the brave
example set his command he saved a large amount of Government property, as well as defeating an insolent and cruel
foe to the country.

After the cessation of hostilities in the South, the
202nd Regiment was sent to the Coal Regions of
Carbon and Schuylkill Counties, and General Albright
placed in command of the Lehigh District, Department of
Pennsylvania. He was mustered out of service with his regiment, in August, 1865.

General Albright is a young man; and a true American
in every sense of the word. An uncompromising and most
ardent lover of freedom and his country, his whole heart was
in the struggle for the preservation of the American Union,
and the free institutions under which its people have pros-
pered. Of indomitable bravery, fine executive ability, and
his highest ambition, being the faithful execution of his duty.
No blemish rests upon the military record of General Charles
Albright.

186TH REG'T. PENNSYLVANIA VOLUNTEERS.

COMPANY "F."

Enlisted February 28, 1864.   Served to the end of the war.

Armbruster, Bartlett
Belsner, August
Eberly, Charles
Glace, Henry
Malley, George

Moore, Robert
Snyder, Wm. R.
Sterling, John
Thomas, Martin
Weyhenmeyer, John

COMPANY "G."

Briggs, Israel
Warner, James,

Johnson, Alexander
Lefler, Layfayette

202ND REG'T PENNSYLVANIA VOLUNTEERS.

Brevet Brigadier-General.—Charles Albright,
> Organized the Regiment in August 1864, and was com-
> missioned Colonel, September 6, 1864. Promoted to Bre-
> vet Brigadier-General, in 1865.

Sergeant-Major.—Oliver Breneiser,*
> Enlisted in Company "F," September 9, 1864. Ap-
> pointed Sergeant-Major, September 7, 1864. Discharged
> August 3, 1865.

COMPANY "A."

[Mustered into the U. S. Service, August 25, 1864, for the term of one
year. Mustered out August 3, 1865.

Captain.—J. D. Laciar, *
First Lieutenant.—Stephen F. Minnick,
Second Lieutenant.—John T. McDaniel,

SERGEANTS.

Josiah Musselman,
Monroe Steigerwalt, *

Tilghman Sittler,
Edward D. Horn.

CORPORALS.

Daniel Kressley, *
Robert Craig, *
George Heister,

William A. Ebert,
John Forgay,
Charles Brey.

Drummer.—Douglas A. Sherry.

PRIVATES.

Beltz, Alexander
Brislin, Cornelius
Becker, James*
Briggs, Samuel C.
Blain, John
Brown, James*
Brown, Philip
Brown, Henry F.*
Boyle, Douglas*
Connaghan, Hugh
Campsie, Thomas*
Campbell, John*
Curran, Mannes*
Callaghan, John
Daubenspeck, Samuel
Drumbore, Henry
Eck, Jonathan*
Fisher, Henry G.
Fisher, Joseph
Focht, Edwin
Frederick, Lewis*
Glace, Edward
Glenn, James
Gombert, Nathan
Hannon, Thomas J.
Hasson, James
Heller, John
Heffelfinger, Joseph
Hollenback, James
Hoyt, Orville E.†
Kissner, William*
Kelley, William
Kelley, Daniel
Kolb, William
Kocher, William
Laggan, James
Lee, Henry*
Leed, William*
Manalis, Condy

Minnick, James
Moulthrop, Jeremiah
Miller, Aaron
Meighan, James
McLaughlin, John
Mulharn, Edward
Mullen, Edward*
McDermott, Patrick
McKeever, Simon
McMurtrie, John A.
Nothstein, Noah
O'Donnell, John
Ott, Levi F.
Popst, Jesse
Poh, Alfred*
Reinheimer, John L.
Reinheimer, Albert
Snyder, Aaron
Smith, Thomas G.
Smith, Jonas
Sleider, Edward
Sensinger, William F.
Solomon, Winfield S.
Sox, Silvaria†
Trausue, Zacharia
Trine, Nathan
Uplinger, Samuel
Vanneman, Asa†
Walton, Charles
Watt, John
Wehr, Owen
Weidaw, Aaron
Williams, Joseph
Williams, William
Williams, Jeremiah
Young, John
Ziegler, Owen
Zellner, Elias
Zink, Tilghman

*) Second enlistment.   †) Recruit.

KILLED AND DIED IN THE SERVICE.

Bachman, Benjamin F.

Died November 11, 1864, in hospital, Alexandria, of wound received in skirmish at Salem, Va., October 8, 1864.

Campbell, William

Died at Mauch Chunk, about September 15, 1864.

Green, Henry

Died at Fairfax Station, Va., December 15, 1864.

Wehr, Lewis

Died in hospital at Alexandria, November 7, 1864.

COMPANY "D."

Ackerman, Albert

Enlisted February, 1865. Served to the end of the war.

Horie, Patrick

Enlisted February, 1865. Served to the end of the war.

Oliver, Ira

Enlisted February, 1865. Served to the end of the war.

Williams, Thomas

Enlisted February. 1865. Served to the end of the war.

COMPANY "I."

Williams, George

Enlisted January 6, 1865. Served to end of the war.

COMPANY "H."

Tudor, James

Enlisted February, 1865. Served to the end of the war.

Loose, Cyrus

Enlisted August, 1864. Served to the end of the war.

COMPANY "E."

Herman, Albert*

Enlisted February, 1865. Served to the end of the war.

Brobst, Frank
Enlisted February, 1865. Served to the end of the war.

COMPANY "F."

Billman, Charles
Enlisted August 31, 1864. Served to end of the war.

Billman, Jonas
Enlisted August 31, 1864. Served to end of the war.

Trainer, Lewis*
Enlisted February 7, 1865. Served to end of the war.

Moulthrop, William H.*
Enlisted February 7, 1865. Served to end of the war.

Schlie, Frederick
Enlisted February 7, 1865. Served to end of the war.

Diehl, Amandus
Enlisted February 7, 1865. Served to end of the war.

Moyer, Daniel
Enlisted February 7, 1865. Served to end of the war.

Bryson, John
Enlisted January 6, 1865. Served to end of the war.

Hough, Joseph
Enlisted January 24, 1865. Served to end of the war.

Deremer, Charles
Enlisted January 6, 1865. Served to end of the war.

Dutter, Charles
Enlisted January 9, 1865. Served to end of the war.

Everett, William
Enlisted January 17, 1865. Served to end of the war.

Klotz, William
Enlisted August 27, 1864. Served to end of the war.

Myers, Franklin
Enlisted January 24, 1865. Served to end of the war.

Pickert, Willoughby
Enlisted September 1, 1864. Served to end of the war.

Smith, Elias
Enlisted September 1, 1864. Served to end of the war.

COMPANY "L."

Enlisted in 1865, and served to disbandonment of the Reg't., Aug. 3, 1865

Radcliff, Thomas   McNamara, Thomas
Boyle, Patrick   Michael, John

Fritzinger, Levi
Sherry, Samuel
George, Joseph F.
Bennyhoff, Joseph
Bostian, Owen T.
Crammer, Jacob
Carl, Peter
Cunnyngham, Francis
Drumbore, Nathan
Farrell, Daniel J.
Hartranft, Simon
McGady, Edward

McCance, Samuel
Martz, Joseph
Moser, Peter
Rex, C. E.
Shaffer, Peter
Klotz, Benjamin
Rouse, John
McLaughlin, John
Swank, Josiah
Hutchison, Marshall
Young, Robert

VOLUNTEER MILITIA OF 1863.

27TH REGIMENT.

[Mustered into service, June 18, 1863.   Discharged, August 5, 1863.]

COMPANY " E."

Sergeant.—C. E. Stedman.
Corporal.—Ed. L. Bullock.

PRIVATES.

Arp, John
Arner, D. D.
Bond, Geo. T.
Brelsford, Henry C.
Bennyhoff, Ed.
Bennyhoff, Joseph
Fister, Wallace B.
Hatrick, Jonathan
Kemerer, M.

Orr, George
Ramsay, Frank
Rutman, Wm.
Rex, C. A.
Siegfried, Henry
Swank, Josiah
Smith, Henry
Xander, A. D.
Zellner, Henry

34TH REG'T. PENN'A. VOLUNTEER MILITIA.

Served during "the Emergency" in June and July, 1863.

Colonel—Charles Albright.

COMPANY "F."

Captain—James Thomas,
First Lieutenant—Thomas Musselman,
Second Lieutenant—Amos Riegel.

SERGEANTS:

1st. Samuel Wolle,   2d. —— Davis,
2d. John Hoff,   4th. Peter Eberts,
    5th. Josiah Musselman,

CORPORALS:

—— Trout,   F. Pettit,
Charles Bowman,   W. B. Anthony,
Charles Seidel,   R. Pfeiffer,
Adam Berlin,   Harrison Kungle.

MUSICIANS:

Charles McDaniel.   Edward Mulharn.

PRIVATES:

Anthony, C. W.	Henry, David
Ashner, Emil	Kuehner, John
Arner, J. H.	Kressley, James
Buck, H.	Kast, F. W.
Buck, D.	Kocher, Wm.
Buck, W.	Leinbach, Willoughby
Banford, W.	Lyons, John
Bloss, ——	Moore, James
Belford, ——	Mattern, Jacob
Beltz, John	Ott, Levi
Billman, Daniel	Pettit, J.
Brey, Charles	Pettit, G.
Beaver, ——	Peters, Henry
Bobst, Charles	Rasp, Christian
Clouse, Granville	Rupp, ——
Cunfer, Gideon	Reinsmith, Nathan
Delaney, ——	Remaley, ——
Dunlap, George	Ramaley, Boas
Eberts, Samuel	Saunder, ——
Eberts, William	Strohl, ——
Eberts, David	Snyder, John
Fritzinger, Levi	Shaeffer. ——
Fertwangler, C.	Semuel, Lewis
Fitzpatrick, ——	Settler, Charles,
Foulke, Wm.	Strouse, Thomas
Grow, Wm.	Swab, ——
Graver, Owen	Trainer, Harrison

Gastin, David
Hunsicker, Joseph
Hoppes, Daniel
Hosler, Frederick
Hand, George
Hill, John

Trine, Nathan
Shoenberger, Wm.
Wertley, John
Weaver, John
Ziegler, Owen
Henry, Christian

COMPANY " A."

Captain.—Jacob Smith.
First Lieutenant.—James Donnelly.
Second Lieutenant.—W. H. Eberly.
Sergeant-Major.—Oliver Breneiser.

SERGEANTS.

First Sergeant.—Josiah W. McCrea.

S. F. Collins,
Cameron Cool,

Edward Hauk,
T. Frank Walter.

CORPORALS.

Nathan Tubbs,
J. Weyhenmeyer,
Thomas H. Ratcliff,
Ezra B. Ely,

C. W. Hamman,
John Sterling,
David H. Butz,
Charles E. Amadon.

MUSICIANS.

Edward D. Horn,

Ed. Remmel.

PRIVATES.

Angle, A. C.
Armbruster, Val.
Barto, Obadiah
Butler, Amos
Brobst, John
Baum, J.
Butler, Robert B.
Beers, Lewis
Beer, J. K.
Bennett, Thomas
Collins, Isaac
Corcoran, Patrick
Cole, Alexander
Dink, John

Leisenring, C. E.
Lance, George
Long, Charles
Leibenguth, Charles
Lockhart, A. H.
Mehan, L. E.
Miller, Philip
Moore, Samuel
Merrick, William
Myer, John A.
Madara, Joseph
Meyers, Jacob
Neith, Frank
Oliver, J. W.

Derbyshire, Henry
Deibert, Andrew
Eberle, C. S. ———
Enbody, Edwin
Esser, George W.
Ehman, Fritz
Ebert, William A.
Gillam, John
Gilbreath, John
Grover, N. M.
Glace, Henry
Gaddes, James
Hutchinson, Marshall
Heilman, William F.
Horn, John
Harlan, William
Holmes, James
Hyndman, Edward
Johnson, Alex.
Kistler, Wilson
Kunkle, William
Kuebler, John
Keiser, Henry
Kramer, Joseph

Rose, George
Siewers, E. R.
Sandhaus, Wm.
Snyder, Wm. R.
Sprowle, George
Smith, P. G.
Smith, A. J.
Seifert, Adam
Strouss, Abraham
Sohl, Henry
Swartwod, John
Stem, Christian
Scip, William
Tobias, A. H.
Ulmstead, Thomas
Unger, Lewis R.
Vanneman, Asa
Valentine, James
Wochter, Thomas
Warner, Edmund
Warner, Wm. S.
Wildoner, J. S.
Warner, James

COMPANY "G."

Captain.—Samuel Harleman.
First Lieutenant.—Sharon McNair.

Brenan, John
Brown, Jeremiah
Buck, Nathan
Blank, Frederick
Coffee, John
Coningham, William
Davis, J. F.
Drombor, Lewis
Dodson, Edward
Eck, Jonathan

Miller, William
Minich, Amos
Roth, A.
Ratz, Baltzer
Roth, L.
Smith, John B.
Sowers, Frank
Severson, Jacob
Smith, Gotlieb
Shelnomer, Samuel

7

Eck, Frank
Fagan, James
Gormly, Smith
Gorman, Eli
Hittler, William
Kishboch, John
Keuhner, Daniel
Keubler, Aaron
Keller, Jacob
Kline, Peter
Kurt, Oliver
Kisthard, Jacob
Karrichner, M.
Leadenham, Henry
Moyer, Noah

Stockley, William
Sitzer, William
Steverson, William
Strohl, Adam
Salin, Lewis W.
Stiles, Lee
Smith, J. W.
Trescolt, L.
Tanny, Samuel
Tanny, Hester
West, G.
Williams, Charles
Watts, James
Weeks, Samuel
Zoll, Nathan

VOLUNTEER MILITIA OF 1862.

19TH REGIMENT.

Colonel.—Robert Klotz.

Captain.—Hiram Wolf.

First Lieutenant.—Thomas R. Crellin.

SERGEANTS.

First Sergeant.—Charles H. Kalbfus,

James Warner,   Allen Craig,
Samuel Patterson,   Charles M. Sweeny.

CORPORALS.

John S. Line,   Dennis H. Dreisbach,
Godfrey Laury,   William Richards,
Alfred Hoffman,   Henry Santee,
Edward Horn,   Chambers Davis.

PRIVATES.

Ely, Benjamin F.   Dick, Charles
Conyngham, Thomas D.   Anthony, George F.
Steadman, Alexander W.   Anthony, William B.
Rex, Charles A.   Bowman, Milton
Hazard, Fisher   Horn, Edward
Esser, George W.   Beel, Joel
Bullock, Edward L.   Laubach, Robert
Enbody, Edward R.   Gower, James
Gaddes, James   Graver, Walter
Steadman, John L.   Saeger, Henry
Dander, Alfred   Dreisbach, Tilghman
Peters, Oliver   Buck, Paul
Lockhart, Cameron   Dreisbach, Lewis
Butler, Robert B.   Solt, Alexander
Bradwell, John   Rehrig, Reuben
Hines, William   Sittler, Tildishman
Harlan, Josiah W.   Hoppes, Daniel
Seifert, Adam   Brown, Charles W.
Loew, Adam   Wolle, Samuel
Whipple, William A.   Davis, George
Hummel, Joseph   O'Brien, David
Cole, Jacob W.   Klotz, Alfred

Strong, James
Ratcliff, Thomas H.
La Rue, Silas H.
Labine, Henry
Swank, Josiah
Shafer, William
Lloyd, John J.
Brislin, John
Frederick, C. D.
Taylor, Edmund
Phifer, Robert
Leffler, Mark L.
Bucks, Henry
Hand, George
Oswalt, August
Reiley, Matthew
Solt, Reuben
Solt, Stephen
Boyer, Jonas
Whitehead, William

Buck, David J.
Solt, Franklin
Dreisbach, Charles
Daubenspeck, Jacob
Daubenspeck, John
Musselman, Josiah
Buck, Charles
Fields, Joseph
Quish, William
Fields, Samuel
Levett, William W.
Best, Stephen
Mentz, Henry W.
Bowman, Oliver O.
Horn, Herman
Rockhill, William P.
Brown, Charles
McConnell, H. H.
Miller, Alexander
Kramer, Theodore W.

MISCELLANEOUS.

COMPANY "C," 183RD REG'T. P. V.

2nd Lieutenant—Samuel Hawk,
Re-enlisted December 11, 1863, as 1st. Sergeant; promoted to 2nd Lieutenant April 16. 1864. Wounded in front of Petersburg, June 16. 1864. Discharged July 3, 1865.

Sergeant—Edward Hawk,
Re-enlisted December 11, 1863. Discharged July 3, '65.

COMPANY "H" 5TH U. S. INFANTRY.

Helshaw, George
Enlisted in 1861. Killed September 1863.

COMPANY "D," 4TH REG'T. VETERAN RESERVES.

Smith, Michael
Enlisted in 1861. Died August 30, 1863.

COMPANY "E," 96TH REGIMENT P. V.

Shædel, Charles
Enlisted in 1861. Died July 2, 1864.

BATTERY "D," 5TH U. S. ARTILLERY.

Williams, David   Warlow, William

COMPANY "H," 98TH REGIMENT P. V.

Folkmer, Charles
Enlisted in 1861. Died May 7, 1864.

COMPANY "A," 96TH REGIMENT P. V.

Rodgers, Alexander
Enlisted in 1861. Died in service.

COEPANY "I," 47TH REGIMENT P. V.

Synder, Jonas

COMPANY "E," 47TH REGIMENT P. V.

Deterline, William
Enlisted in 1861. Served three years.

116TH REGIMENT VET. P. V.

Hosler, Frederick
Enlisted in 1864.   Served to the end of the war.

Kressley, James
Enlisted in 1864.   Served to the end of the war.

Steigerwalt, Lewis
Enlisted in 1864.   Served to the end of the war.

48TH REIMENT VET. P. V.

West, Edward R.
Enlisted in 1861.   Re-enlisted in 1863, and served to the end of the war.

1ST NEW JERSEY VOLUNTEERS.

Warner, John
Enlisted in 1861.   Served to the end of the war.

COMPANY "I," 118TH REGIMENT P. V.

Enbody, Robert
Enlisted November 17, 1863.   Taken prisoner at Cold Harbor, June 2, 1864.   In prison at Andersonville to December 10, 1864.   Discharged May 1, 1865.

COMPANY "A," 35TH NEW JERSEY VOLUNTEERS.

Beckhardt, Joseph
Enlisted August 19, 1863.   Served to end of the war.

COMPANY "G," 68TH REG'T. NEW YORK VOLS.

Patterson, James
Enlisted in 1864.   Killed at the battle of the Wilderness May 3, 1864.

COMPANY "A," 109TH REG'T. P. V.

Davidson, Daniel
Died in service.

COMPANY "F," 148TH REG'T. P. V.

Wells, John
Killed in battle.

COMPANY "C," 50TH REG'T. P. V.

Fahl, Richard

COMPANY "C," 6TH PENN'A. CAVALRY.

Boyle, Charles
Enlisted in 1861. Killed at the battle of Fredericksburg,
July 5, 1863.

201ST REGIMENT PENN'A. VOLS.

Horn, John
Enlisted in February 1865.   Discharged at the close of
the war.

6TH REGIMENT PENN'A. CAVALRY.

Ginder, Jacob
Enlisted March 7, 1865,—having served three years in
the 81st Regt. P. V.

Neith, Frank
Enlisted March 7, 1865.   Served to the end of the war.

129TH REGIMENT P. V.

Ormrod, William
Enlisted August 1862.   Served nine months.

Luckenbach, Edward F.
Enlisted August 1862.   Served nine months.

72ND REGIMENT PENN'A. VOLUNTEERS.

Brown, Henry F.
Enlisted in 1861.   Honorably discharged in 1863, on account of disability.

73RD REGIMENT PENN'A. VOLS.

Wehley, Jerome
Enlisted in 1861.   Appointed chief Bugler. Discharged
by order of the War Department in 186?.

COMPANY "C," 35TH NEW JERSEY VOLS.

Derbyshire, James
Enlisted October 1864.   Served to the end of the war.

COMPANY "A," 10TH NEW JERSEY VOLUNTEERS.

McIntosh, George
> Enlisted 1864. Captured at the battle of the Wilderness.
> May 3, 1864. Discharged at the end of the war.

NAVY.

Cooper, Charles
> Entered service as an Assistant Engineer. Served to the end of the war.

Faga, Nathan,
> Seaman. Served to end of the war.

COMPANY "I," 199TH REGIMENT P. V.

Eshman, Joseph
> Enlisted August 16, 1864. Served to end of the war

Koons, Joseph
> Enlisted August 16, 1864. Served to end of the war

Paltzgrove, William
> Enlisted August 16, 1864. Served to end of the war.

Schnell, Reuben
> Enlisted August 16, 1864. Served to end of the war.

COMPANY "G," 47TH REG'T P. V.

Deterline, Timothy
> Enlisted in 1864. Served to the end of the war.

Faust, Malrie
> Enlisted in 1864. Served to the end of the war.

Graver, John (Co. B.)
> Enlisted in 1864. Served to the end of the war.

3RD NEW JERSEY CAVALRY.

Buel, Charles
> Enlisted in 1864. Served to the end of the war.

COMPANY "K," 54TH REG'T. P. V.

Rehrig, George
> Enlisted February 15, 1864.

OOMPANY "B," 11TH REG'T. P. V.

Clark, Geo. E. A.
> Enlisted August 19, 1861. Re-enlisted November 1, '63.
> Transferred to Co. C, 188th Regt. P. V., May 4, 1864, and
> served to the end of the war.

COMPANY "C," 188TH REGIMENT P. V.

Beers, Joel
> Enlisted in 1864. Served to the end of the war.

COMPANY "H," 209TH REG'T. P. V.

Klotz, Jonathan
> Enlisted in 1864. Wounded in front of Petersburg,
> March 25, 1865. Died of his wounds three days later

COL. JAMES MILLER.

This is a name that will live long in the annals of Carbon County. So long as a spark of patriotism burns in the hearts of our people ; so long as deeds of heroism, patriotic devotion to country, and true soldierly and gentlemanly qualities are appreciated, so long will the name and memory of Colonel Miller be remembered in Carbon County. He fell, an early victim to the accursed rebellion which slayed thousands of the best and truest men of the country.

Col. Miller was born in South Easton in the year 1825.— When quite a youth, he removed from Easton to Mauch Chunk, and established himself in business. He became a member of the Stockton Artillerists, when first organized by Captain John Leisenring, and when the Mexican War broke out in 1846, he raised a company based upon the Stockton Artillerists, and bearing that name. The company marched from Mauch Chunk on the 24th of December, 1846, and at Pittsburg were attached to the 2nd Regiment of Volunteers, Col. Roberts. From this point they went *via* the Ohio and Mississippi, to Mexico, and joined Gen. Scott's army before Vera Cruz.

Captain Miller was subsequently engaged in every battle from Vera Cruz to the City of Mexico. At the battle of Chepultepec, Capt. Miller was selected by Gen. Quitman to join Major Twiggs, who had a separate command of 240 picked men, constituting the storming party of the Division. The day previous to the storming of Chepultepec, the storming party were engaged in important reconnoisances in front of the enemy's works, the result of which led to the discovery of the position of the enemy's strongest batteries. On the morning of the 13th of September, at the dawn of day, the storming party were moved out in front of the Division.— The number of Captain Miller's men had been reduced, by casualties, to twenty-six.

Before reaching the base of Chepultepec, Major Twiggs

was disabled and his party severely cut up. After the fall of Major Twiggs, the command devolved upon Captain Miller, who, though himself wounded, led the assaulting party to the castle of Chepultepec. Captain Miller's command were among the first to enter. More than half the party were either killed or wounded. From thence battery after battery was stormed, until they reached the gates of the city, Capt. Miller still in command.

Upon the breaking out of the rebellion, Col. Miller, who was then engaged in the coal business in New York, returned to Carbon County, and commenced the organization of the " Chippewa Regiment,"—the 81st Penn'a. Vols., and was commissioned Colonel. The subsequent record of this regiment shows that it was one of the very best and most reliable regiments in the United States service. Col. Miller was a severe disciplinarian ; fearless, impulsive, totally regardless of personal considerations in the discharge of duties, he was always at the post of danger.

He was killed at the battle of Fair Oaks, June 1, 1862, the first battle in which his regiment participated. Had he been spared to the country, there is but little doubt but that he would have attained high rank.

COL. JOHN D. BERTOLETTE,

Entered the service April 21st, 1861, as 2nd Lieutenant of Company A, 6th Reg't. Penn'a. Vols. Promoted to 1st Lieutenant and Adjutant, May 1, 1861. Mustered out with the Regiment July 28, 1861. Re-enlisted August 20, 1861, as 1st Lieutenant and Adjutant of the 48th Regiment Penna. Vols. Served with his regiment until April 23rd, 1862, when he was appointed A. A. A. G. on Gen. James Nagle's staff, commanding First Brigade, 2nd Division, Department of

North Carolina. On the 25th of September, 1862, he was appointed by President Lincoln, Assistant Adjutant General of Volunteers, with the rank of Captain. Promoted Major by brevet, December 2nd, 1864, "for gallant and distinguished services at the battles of Poplar Grove Church, Hatcher's Run, and during the campaign before Richmond, Va." Promoted to Lieutenant-Colonel by brevet, March 25, 1865, "for gallantry and distinguished services at Fort Steadman, Va." Promoted to Colonel by brevet, April 2nd, 1865, "for gallant and meritorious services in the assault upon the enemy's lines in front of Fort Sedgwick, Va." Col. Bertolette was severely wounded in the battle of Bull Run, August 29, 1862, then serving on Gen. Nagle's Staff.

There is probably no soldier in the State of Colonel Bertolette's rank who has a fairer record, or who served his country more faithfully during the rebellion. He was repeatedly highly complimented in General Orders, for bravery and gallant conduct in battle.

DRAFTED MEN FOR NINE MONTHS.

The following is a complete list of the men drafted in Carbon County for nine months in 1862. It is but proper to say that the enrollment was a very imperfect one, and that this roll includes men who were then in the army ; and also many aliens.

LOWER TOWAMENSING.

Andrew, Joseph, Jr.
*Andrew, Edward
Boyer, David
Beahler, Daniel
Beahler, Jacob
Beahler, Levi
Christman, Stephen
Cossler, William
Dailing, Henry
Dunbar, Robert
Fowl, Peter
Greenzweig, William
Klotz, Levi
Keiner, Reuben

Knappenberger, A.
Leesman, Augustus
Lauer, Henry
Mehrkaum, Charles
Reinhard, Lewis
Snyder, David
Smith, Lewis
Snyder, Thomas
Strouss, Daniel
Serfass, Daniel, Jr.
Seltzer, John
Smith, L.
Schultz, Lewis
Vogel, Stephen.

FRANKLIN TOWNSHIP.

Aschner, Emill
Bauer, John F.
Heberling, D. C.
Hartman, Alexander
Larish, James
Master, Adam

Markley, Stephen
Palsgrove, C. J.
Schmoyer, Israel
Sweirer, Matthew
Solt, Alexander
Zimmerman, David.

LAUSANNE TOWNSHIP.

Byran, James
Clingh, Israel
Dakin, John
Gangwere, Samuel
Guckavan, William
Harvey, Thomas

Hoff, Josiah
Kirk, William
McMurtrie, John
McMurtrie, Michael
Shafer, John
Woodring, George
Walsh, James.

PACKER TOWNSHIP.

Foust Daniel
Neifort, Moses

Steward, D. L.
Young, Edwin.

EAST PENN TOWNSHIP.

Freeby, Solomon
Halliner, Charles
Kreitz, John. Jr.
Knecht, Samuel
Miller, John
Nothstein, Jonas

Ruch, Thomas
Steigewalt, Levi
Steigewalt, Moses
Smith, Owen
Weidaw, Benjamin
Zellner, Elias.

BANKS TOWNSHIP.

Bennett, Stephen
Bohlender, Antony
Boyle, John
Brown, John
Boyle, Barney
Bush, Samuel
Charles, William
Call, James
Donahoe, Thomas O.
Donahoe, Matthew
Dempsy, James
Dugan, Charles
Davis, John D.
Francis, John
Ganghen, Michael
Goucher, Thomas
Gallagher, Patrick
Hooven, E. F.
Hess, Valentine

Hoyt, D. W.
Hurdwick, Adam
Horn, John
Icifetter, Lewis
James, Edwin
Kroft, Henry
Loch Samuel
Mulhenen, Dennis
McNulty, John
McBrearty, Patrick
Maloy, Barney
McCole, J. H.
Orey, Robert
Pratt, Jacob
Spade, Benedict
Smith, John W.
Tweedle, Richard
Woolfram, Charles
Walsh, Frank

Yost Newton C.

TOWAMENSING TOWNSHIP.

Beer, George
Beer, Conrad
Christman, Nathan
Distler, John
Eckhard, Abraham

Greensweig, Joseph
Greensweig, Samuel
Henger, Antony
Jones, William
McDaniel, Robert

Nepp, Casper.

DRAFT OF 1863 FOR THREE YEARS.

BANKS TOWNSHIP.

Arnold, John
Boyle, Edward
Boyle, Barney 1st
Brady, Henry
Brislin, Hugh
Broderick, John
Brown, John E.
Burke, Thomas
Boyle, Barney 2nd
Butley, Martin
Brittain, John
Boyle, Hugh 3rd
Burns, Patrick
Boyle, John
Beck, George
Boyle, Hugh 1st
Bardy, Patrick
Berger, F.
Banks, Lawrence
Brill, Phillip
Boyce, James
Betz, Martin
Brisslin, Edward
Berger, John
Boyle, Barney 3rd
Carey, John
Clayton, Richard
Cannon, Patrick
Corran, Edward
Cononingham, Robert
Cullin, John
Cannon, Hugh
Campbell, M.
Dolan, John
Dintinger, Jacob
Dougherty, William
Dugan, Hugh No. 2.
Dougherty, John
Davis, David

Haycock, Thomas
Harkins, James
Hughs, William
Henry, Jonas
Hill, Joseph
Kelley, Dennis
Kuhn, Charles
Kropp, John
Lowenstein, Moses
Lynch, Charles
Lauer, Jacob
McCafferty, Daniel
Maloy, Amandes
Mulligan, Daniel
McDonald, John
McPhelps, Michael
McGee, Owen
McFadden, Barney
McNallis, Edward
Maley, Patrick
McHugh, Antony
Metcalf, Simon
McShay, Thomas
Mooney, John
Maloney, Patrick
McHugh, Daniel
Maxey John
Meyers, F.
McCann, Michael
McBride, John
McCurley, James
Mulligan, John
Martin, John
Matthews, Thomas
McGinley, Neal
McLafferty, James
Noteries, M.
O'Donald, M.
O'Donald, Frank

Dougherty, Neal
Dougherty, Arthur No. 1.
Dougherty, Arthur No. 2.
Dugan, Daniel
Dergan, Owen
Davis, John D.
Dougherty, Richard
Donahue, John
Edwards, Edward
Evans, David J.
Fisher, C.
Fall, William
Fessler, Levi
Frey, John E.
Fannycase, Thomas
Grisswold, Morgan
Grunewald, Jacob
Gallagher, John No. 5.
Gates, Joseph
Glenhorn, C.
Gallow, Jack
Gallagher, John No. 4.
Gallagher, C.
Gaushin, James
Gallagher, Owen
Geusel, Daniel
Harrity, Hugh
Haudel, Charles
Horlacher, J. P. C.
Haycock, Reiser

Prosser, Benjamin
Prosser, John
Purcel, James
Quade, Frank H.
Roberts, A. W.
Roab, George
Reed Robert
Rogers, James
Rymiller, George
Speidel, William
Sweeney, Thomas
Stonebach, Henry
Sharkey, Peter
Stewart, John L.
Schovel, Peter
Sharkey, John
Sweeney, James
Schmerr, Phillip
Shovelin, Peter
Seeger, John
Tweedel, James
Thomas, Lewis
Thomas, Z.
Tweedel, J. B.
Tweedel, Thomas
Whalig, Michael
Watson, James
Wear, John
Ward, Thomas
Zneller, Joseph

EAST MAUCH CHUNK.

Branman, Charles
Boyle, James
Blakslee, R. K.
Boyle, Michael
Bower, Fred.
Buckman, Samuel
Connaghan, Hugh
Conner, John
Deichman, John
Dugan, A.

Klotz, Edward
McGee, John
McGee, Patrick
Miller, John
McGrady, John
McGee, Charles
Michael, Jacob
McGee, Daniel
Oustrode, Jeremiah
O'Donnell, Neal

Detweiler, Tilghman
Forman, Christian
Flood, James
Gallagher, Charles
Harkin, James
Hines, Andrew
Kennedy, Samuel

Ruth, Manassas
Rice, Enoch
Stetler, David
Smith, Peter P.
Seabach, Fred.
Swartz, David
Thompson, William

EAST PENN TOWNSHIP.

Andreas,
Bechtel, David
Cox, Nathan
Fink, Reuben
Ginder, Lewis
Holshoe, Joseph
Holshoe, David

Jones, D. G.
Kolb, Nathan
Mertz, Henry
Miller, Lewis A.
Neff, Reuben
Romeck, Ephraim
Rahrig, Martin R.
Walt, Daniel

Ruch, Jacob jr.
Rex, Moses
Rahrig, Lewis H.
Steigerwalt, Joshua
Steigerwalt, Jacob
Schock, Joseph
Smith, Owen

FRANKLIN TOWNSHIP.

Anthony, George F.
Bauman, John
Beltz, John F.
Brunner, John
Boyer, Benjamin
Bartolet, Benj.
Boyer, George
Buck, Joseph
Clampfer, William
Deibert, Jonathan
Davis, George
Davidson, David
Graul, Wm.
Graver, Jacob
Gilham, John
Hartman, David

Keck, Benj.
Kromer, Edward
Loveitt, William
Montz, Nathan
Mohr, William
Mertz, Frank
Mengold, Fred.
Pheifer, Jacob
Reinart, Peter
Reinart, Solomon
Rehrig, Cornelius
Ruch, John
Rhoads, S. G.,
(Preacher.)
Reinart, Simon
Strohl, James

Stroup, Jacob
Solt, Lewis
Schnell, Reuben
Stout, Alexander
Schreiber, Lewis
Shirer, Stephen
Schwaup, Charles
Sensinger, Edwin
Wentz, Dennis
Walk, Edward
Walk, David
Wurtely, J. No. 1.
Wurtely, J. No. 2.
Youndt, Francis
Zimmerman, Reub.

KIDDER TOWNSHIP.

Albee, James E.
Benninger, Henry
Baler, Simon
Bore, Nicholas
Benson, Michael

Fradle, Timothy
Garman, Patrick
Goden, Frank
Gillie, P. H.
Hilliard, Samuel

Macas, John
Meredith, Timothy
McLarry, Wm.
Morris, F. B.
Mixsell, Henry

8

Curry, Anthony
Callahan, John
Collier, Dan. No. 1.
Collier, Dan. No. 2.
Cole, Jacob
Degman, Chas.
Dodd, Thomas
Davidson, Simon
Eller, Jacob
Finnan, Mike
Fess, George

Hauck, Timothy
Heinbach, Harri'n
Herdmeker, J. G.
Kronan, John
Kelly, James
Knecht Alvin. H.
Kane, James
Long, John D.
Lamarey, Philip
McCarty, Samuel
Morris, W. C.
West, Levi

Morsh, Christian
Parks, Wm. R.
Ryan, William
Spragen, Augustus
Sholten, Lewis
Shine, Daniel
Steiner, Jacob
Shafer, Hugh J. O.
Sharry, Samuel
Sheeter, William
Walten, Sylvester

LAUSANNE TOWNSHIP.

Balliet, N. V.
Carrigan, Michael
Clark, William
Derr, Abraham
Dougherty, John
Derr, Paul
Farley, Francis
Garis, James R.
Gangwer, Wm.
Gorden, Wm. J.
Hamlin, Joseph
Hufford, Francis
Harts, Abraham
Hill, Edward
Hay, Peter
Harkman, Samuel
Hooven, H. A.
Hamlin, Edward

Kisthatt, Jacob
Kishbach, Levi
Kline, Peter
Kuehler, Aaron
Kromer, M. G.
Kishbach, John
Kernan, James
Kelly, Stephen
Keiner, Augustus
Lachner, Jacob
Martz, Frank
Minnich, Amos
McDermott, F. J.
Markey, Edward
McNeil, D. A.
Need, William
Neronan, P.
(R. C. Preacher,)

Parker, John
Picket, Frederick
Roath, Andrew
Rehrig, Joseph
Rudder, Thomas
Roads, Lewis
Sowers, Franklin
Stokes, Marx
Shellhammer, David
Stetler, George
Salen, Lewis
Sackett, W. W.
Spanner, James
Stewart, James
Simmons, Samuel
Stiles, W. L.
Tourney, John
Williams, H. B.

MAHONING TOWNSHIP.

Beltz, Isaac
Cooper, Chas.
Dontzman, Stephen
Derbyshire, Henry
Evarts, David
Farren, Chas.
Flickenger, Reuben
Fryman, Thomas

Klotz, Silas
Moyer, Joseph
Murphy, George
Musselman, Josiah
McLean, Thomas
Mentz, William
Moyer,   "
Nesley,   "

Schmidt, Lewis
Sweeny, Chas. W.
Steigerwaldt, Daniel
Strouss, Thomas
Schoch, Daniel
Snyder, Phaon
Sandel, Alex.
Srouss, Jacob

Fritz, Daniel
Frailich, Chas.
Fuhrer, William
Graver, Samuel
Green, George
Grosbaum, Samuel
Houtz, Nathaniel
Hoon, Thomas
Kromer, William
Kistler, William
Kitzler, John

Neibert, John
Probst, Daniel
Patterson, A. L.
Raudenbush, J. W.
Ramaly, Stephen
Raric, Lewis
Rhoads, William
Raric, Noah
Reiber, Nathaniel B.
Rex, Moses
Singart, Robert

Snyder, Samuel
Shively, Franklin
Trumbour, Alfred
Watson, Samuel W.
Weiss, William
Weidaw, Aaron
Weiss, Nero
Werth, Willoughby
Zellner, Henry
Zehn, Joseph

MAUCH CHUNK BOROUGH.

Adams, John
Anthony, Michael
Brodhead, R. M.
Blakslee, E. H.
Bunting, Dr. T. C.
Bastian, O. S.
Barto, Obadiah
Brown, Chas.
Brower, R. E.
Behee, John
Bertch, D. G.
Bryson, Daniel
Barron, John
Bruns, Dan. jr.
Bertsch, Daniel
Corby, Joseph
Church, Ira
Cummins, Jona.
Chapman, Wm.
Dunlap, Wm.
Dodson, John
Dottes, Daniel
Deitz, John
Dugan, Patrick
Esser, George W.
Ely, Ezra B.
Ehman, Fritz
Flentze, Dr. L.
Ferry, Chas.
Fellows, A. W.

Fried, Neal
Griffin, Patrick
Gable, Nelby
Haines, August
Handy, N. F.
Heberling, James
Hyndman, M. B.
Houpt, Moses
Hinkle, Joshua
Hoats, Morgan
Hess, Henry
Johnson, Thomas
Kettera, John
Kistler, Wilson
Kurtz, Godfrey
Keifer, Paul jr.
Lahr, Ezra
Laman, Andrew
Miller, James
Marrion, Andrew
McGeady, John jr.
McGinley, Edw.
Moore, Samuel
Miller, Charles
McCall, Luke
Maloy, Patrick
McIntosh, Wallace
McGinly, John
Mercur, Fred.
McFadden, D.

Ott, Henry
Oliver, John
Patterson, Samuel
Packer, Robert A.
Peters, Joseph
Pryor, James
Riegel, Joshua
Ruff, George
Steckel, Edw. M.
Storm, Lewis
Sandherr, William
Strauss, Alvin
Seip, Ferdinand
Steadman, Jno. L.
Sherry, Samuel
Smith, John
Swartwood, John
Smith, Peter
Tacey, Joseph P.
Walters, Wm.
Ward, Adam
Wilhelm, James H.
Wilhelm, Geo. W.
Wilke, Henry
Wingard, E. B.
Ward, Daniel
Wolf, Adolph
Young, George
Yagle, Amandes

NESQUEHONING TOWNSHIP.

Cadden, Patrick
Cawllen, Thomas
Duffy, Patrick
Hendrick, Edg. L.
Hackett, William

Kindder, John
McCabe, Hugh
McDonnell, Tho.
McDonald, G. W.
McLeslie, Samuel

Smitham, Richard
Stevens, Isaac
Wolbert, Jacob
Watkins, Wm.

PACKER TOWNSHIP.

Arner, Moses
Foust, John jr.
Gerhart, Levi

Hartz, David
Krap, Casper
Neifert, Martin

Wetzell, Samuel
Wetzell, David
Wetzell, Aaron

PENN FOREST TOWNSHIP.

Becker, Bevy
Brown, Fred.
Campbell, Wm.
Cortright, Henry
Clingesine, John
Donnelly, Peter
Finnegan, Thomas
Griffin, John
Halten, James
Haws, Frederick

Knes, Owen
Keiper, Nathan
Lanyer, Francis
Linebacher, Henry
Merwes, Herman
Mackes, S. W.
McCue, Thomas
Pryor, James
Stonehouse, Fred.
Snyder, David
Yerger, Solomon

Serfass, Jacob
Serfas Wilson
Snyder, William
Sherry Henry
Shorter, Patrick,
Smith, Franklin
Strohl, Thomas
Shiffer, Stenard
Serfass, Reuben
Serfass, Aaron

SUMMIT HILL.

Argus, Henry
Alexander, Robert
Boyd, Wm. 2d
Boyle, James
Beltz, Thomas
Birmingham, Edw.
Boyle, Jas. D.
Bacon, Henry
Brislin, John
Boyle, Thomas
Caldwell, John
Carrigan, Hugh
Campbell, John
Campbell, Wm.
Crowe, Wm.
Connelly, Owen jr.

Gallagher, Chas.
Gallagher, Jno. 1st
Gallagher, Jno. 2d
Harkins, Hugh
Hughes, David
Harris, John P.
Halsey, Wm. K.
Hogg, Samuel
Harrington, John
Hannon, Thomas J.
Hoover, Thomas
Heffelfinger, J. J.
Jones, Morgan
James, Henry C.
Keenahan, James
Kemerer, Mahlon

McHugh, James
McMichael, Daniel
McDonnel, Patrick
McLaughlin, Wm.
McCool, Cornelius
Maloy, Charles
McFeely, James
Neyer, Thomas
O'Donnel, Domi.
O'Donnel, Jno. 3d
Pollock, Thomas
Prosser, John T.
Pollock, Samuel
Phillips, George
Quigley, Michael
Rafter, John

Cannen, Daniel
Donahue, James
Drophy, Peter
Davis, Thomas D.
Dreisbach, Elas
Davis, John
Erwin, Matthew
Edwards, Richard
Evans, Frank
Early, Wm.
Early, Alexander
Fisher, Patrick
Frey, Charles
Fleming, Smith
Fisher, Owen
Fritz, Reuben F.
Fisher, Wm.
Gallagher, Frank
Galler, John (9th)
Griffith, David
Gallagher, Jas. S.

Kennedy, Cor.
Kennan, Andrew
Kale, Jacob
Kelley, Thomas
Kennedy, Dan. 2d
Lewis, John
Morton, Jacob
McTague, Thomas
Maley, James
Miller, Jeremiah
McMichael, John
Minnick, Edward
McGee, James
Malley, Daniel
Miller, Wm. 1st
Miller, Wm. 2d
Martin, Jacob
Murphey, James
Maloy, John
Moser, Abraham
Moore, Edward

Ross, James
Rodgers, Edward
Rickert, Solomon
Shirey, Samuel
Shields, Francis
Sommers, Thomas
Shovelin, Cornelius
Stephenson, Joseph
Smith, Edwin
Swank, Wm.
Shinton, Thomas
Sharpe, Peter
Sharpe, Charles
Thompson, Wm.
Van Horn, Alex.
Wintersteen, Phil.
Webler, Edward
Ward, Michael
Wilmot, George
Zehner, Charles

TOWAMENSING TOWNSHIP.

Beer, Joseph
Beer, Joel
Buck, William
Beer Benjamin
Beer, John
Beer, Samuel

Christman, Wm.
Eckert, Abraham
Eckert, Joseph
Greensweig, H.
Greensweig, Joseph
Kerney, Samuel

Strohl, Wm.
Stemler, Reuben
Shoenberger, Wm.
Smith, Paul
Smith, Nathan
Scheffer, Thomas

LOWER TOWAMENSING TOWNSHIP.

Andrew, Edward
Beer, Alexander
Boyer, Edward
Beltz, Joseph
Beltz, William
Bartholomew, Jac.
Bloss, Wm.
Bebbeet, Charles
Beinart, James
Bower, John
Behler, Levi
Bloss, Daniel jr.
Farber, Reuben
Graff, Lewis

George, John
George, Daniel
George, Charles
Goodheil, John
Klotz, Charles
Klotz, Levi
Klotz, Charles
Kern, Peter
Kline, Jacob
Kunkle, George
Leffler, Jacob
Lawer, Wm.
McFarland, Henry
Mehrkamm, John

Ramaley, Lafayette
Reiss, Tilghman
Ramaley, Henry
Strawberger, Mat.
Selser, John
Smith, Daniel
Sherrer, Wm.
Strold, Henry
Straub, John
Selfies, Charles
Snyder, Wash.
Souders, William
Snyder, Reuben
Thompson, George

Greensweig, Adam   Meges, Joel   Wannemacher, Per.
Getz, Tobias   Ramaley, Daniel

DRAFTED JUNE 13, 1864, FOR THREE YEARS.

BANKS TOWNSHIP.

Acker, Benneville   Gallagher, Tague   McDarraugh Jas.
Boyle, Hugh 1st   Gallagher, Owen   McHenry, Stephen
Boyle, Hugh 2d   Giser, Phillip   McFadden, J. 1st
Brislin, Hugh   Gonchin, Michael   McCollum, J. K.
Burns, Felix   Gatens, Martin   McGeady, John
Berger, Fred.   Gonchin, Thomas   McBride, James
Boyle, Condy   Hudson, Price   Phelp, William
Boyle, Edward   Hoff, John   Penser, "
Boyle, Dennis   Haycock, Reese   Reneer, "
Bender, Samuel   Hines, John   Reynolds, John
Burkhart, John   Highland, Edw.   Reiley, George
Brannan, Martin   Henry, David   Roberts, J. K
Boyle, Barny 1st   Johnson, James   Schovel, Jacob
Coll, Daniel   Korer, Alexander   Sharp, John 1st
Crary, Mason B.   Kelley, Edward   Stoneback, Henry
Carey, John   Kropp, John   Skelton, John
Cooper, Luke   Longshore, John   Sweeney, John 1st
Duffy, Charles   Moore, Michael   Shoup, Peter
Didium, John   Moony, Hugh   Shaffer, Casper
Dougherty, Richard   McGee, James   Sweeney, Patrick
Davis, Wm. D.   McNulty, John 2d   Smith, Hugh
Dugan, James   McGee, John   Spatzer, Emanuel
Dugan, Barney   McBrearty, Barny   Swob, Peter
Evans, Daniel   Maley, Patrick   Tomminey, Peter
Fitch, Anthony   McNulty, Daniel   Troy, Daniel
Fowler, M. D.   Maloy, Barney   Thorpe, John
Friele, John   Mumper, A. L.   Weber, "
Ferry, John 1st   McCafferty, John   Ward, Patrick
Farrow, Levi   McHugh, Connel   Wegan, George
Ferry, John   Murray, Charles   Whalen, Michael
Fritz, George   McGee, Connelly   Welsh, Francis
Gallagher, Condy   McEnnelly, Patrick   Woodring, Nich.

EAST MAUCH CHUNK.

Brown, Joseph   Gausler, John   Mentz, Sebastian
Brodhead, Daniel   Gallagher, Joseph   Muckley, Henry
Byleman, Henry   Gallagher, Daniel   McCoal, Neal
Brodhead, A. J.   Gallagher, Patrick   McQuare, James 2d

Burk, Martin
Brady, Charles
Brady, John
Bennehoff, Jonas
Connaghan, Hugh
Ebert, Nathan
Griffin, George

Houtz, Hiram
Harkins, Edward
Kuehner, Thomas
McGee, John
McGady, Daniel
Miller, Fred.
Miller, Andrew

McNelas, Neal
Root, Manasses
Rough, Henry
Skelley Patrick
Sweeney, Daniel
Treharn, David
Thomas, Josiah

EAST PENN TOWNSHIP.

Bailey, Daniel
Frieley, Solomon
Hoffman, Samuel

Holshue, Joseph
Kistler, D. W.
Peter, Godfrey
Smith, Elias

Serfass, Henry
Steigerwalt, Stephen
Schmith, Owen

KIDDER TOWNSHIP.

Baldwin, Thomas
Bell, William
Brakely Matthias
Blakeslee, Chas.
Cole, Jacob
Donnel, Peter
Dun, Mike
Dutter, Reuben
Dolan, Patrick

Eckerd, John
Edleman, John T.
Frable, Conrad
Hale, M. D.
Kresge, Amandus
Kern, William
Kresge, Lyman
Miksell, Henry
McName, Turner
West, Levi

Makes, John
Nanny, Peter
Neely, Wm.
Smith, John
Seer, Levi
Scholifield, John
Toomy, John
Welch, Thomas
Winters, Tip

NESQUEHONING TOWNSHIP.

Burns, Edward
Cox, John
Clark, Michael
Coyle, Terrance
Crossen, Owen

Clark, Thomas
Donahoe, John
Duffy, Francis
Fisher, Isaac
Holmes, Chas.
Smith, Thomas

Jenkins, Morgan
Leslie, John
McCarrell, James
Riley, Hugh
Reese, David

PACKER TOWNSHIP.

Arner, Thomas
Backert, Henry
Clanigan, John
Englehart, John

Gerhardt, Daniel
Hinkle, Amos
Moses, John
Nace, Jacob
Young, G. W.

Rinker, John
Rinker, Solomon
Romig, John
Woodlin, John

PENN FOREST TOWNSHIP.

Agley, George
Almanecker, John
Breamer, Chas.
Bugher, Amos

Donahoe, Patrick
Green, Michael
Mooney, Michael
Prutzman, David

Righter, George
Serfass, Lewis
Stinehart, S. Girard.

LAUSANNE TOWNSHIP.

Bryan, John
Bauchman, G. H.
Becker, Jacob
Bannon, James
Berkhard, Edw.
Carroll, Charles
Deterline, Wm.
Davis, John
Dunnson, Patrick
Dunnigan, James
Eddie, James
Eck, Franklin
Eams, Joseph
Eck, Paul
Gibbon, Wm.
Harleman, Thomas
Hend, Bernard
Hackett, Thomas

Hetinger, Lewis
King, J. R.
Kirk, Wm.
Kisthard,
Keener, Daniel
Kingle, Lewis
Laughran, Owen
Lamon, Henry
Leadenham, Henry
Lunger, Wm.
McCabe, John
McGee, Daniel
Maginty, Mannes
Miller, Joseph
McCluskey, Chas.
McGinty, Edward
O'Donnell, John C.
Picket, Wm.

Reed, Henry
Rase, Frederick
Rems, James
Rudden, John
Smith, J. W.
Stevenson, Wm.
Terns, Thomas
Trumble, Lewis
Wilcrout, Solomon
Weiss, Charles
Winn, Michael
Watson, Newton
Ward, Condy
Weiss, J. A.
Webster, Flem
Ward, Patrick
Wilson, John
Watts, James

SUMMIT HILL.

Abbott, Robert
Botts, Philip
Brislin, Patrick
Beltz, Harrison
Boyd, Wm. 2d
Beltz, Charles
Boyd, Robert
Brislin, James
Boyle, Dennis 2d
Boner, Condy
Caregan, Michael
Campbell, Henry
Courtright, W. B.
Conaghan, James W.
Downs, Thomas
Dougherty, Patrick
Diver, Thomas
Davis, David P.
Dougherty, Aaron
Dale, Samuel
Fringenown, Wm.
Fleming, Smith
Fagan, James
Fink, Lawrence

Fisher, Caleb
Finley, James
Gallagher, John 7th
Gazton, David
Griffith, Benjamin
Gallagher, James
Houser, Nathan
Haycock John
Harran, Edw.
Harkins, James
Howard, David
Harkins, Hugh 2d
Jones, Morgan
Klace, Joseph
Kelly, Charles
Kennedy, Hugh
Lewis, John
Lewis, Wm. T.
Lynch, Richmond
McGill, Terrence
May, John
Musselman, Josiah
Maloy, James
McLaughlin, John

Mulherron, Michael
Miller, Peter
McGilloway, James
Miller, Alexander
Mauser, J. B.
Moore, Peter
McGee, Patrick
Martin, Monroe
McFadden, John
Nevins, Samuel
Nevins, Joseph
Oliver, Samuel
Pollock, Samuel
Ponting, Thomas
Pollock, Benj. R.
Roberts, Jacob, jr.,
Redline, Abraham
Starch, Philip
Stout, Manasses
Sharp, Condy
Scott, James
Storch, Henry
Welsh, Patrick
Williams, Josiah